The Animating Presence

...the One...everywhere present...

Mary Saint-Marie
Sheoekah Amu

Published by Ancient Beauty Studios,   www.marysaintmarie.com

ISBN: 978-0-9646572-0-5 (sc)

All artwork by Mary Saint-Marie

Cover Art: *The Rainbow Dream of Beauty-SHE...*

> *I do dwell ever in a place...*
> *where inward...is outward...*
> *a place where directions cease to be...*
> *a place where the rainbow...*
> *is a glow of white...*

Book Design and Layout by Aaron Rose, Mount Shasta, California

Other publications by Mary Saint-Marie:
Galactic Shamanism
The Holy Sight
Messages from the Silence
Nectar of Woman
The Sacred Two
The Star-Stone Ones

Dedication

This book is dedicated to the animating presence.

Passages

Acknowledgments

Each time a book arises in my consciousness and I look at whom I will thank, the list is really too long to include all and everything.

Each greeting, each meeting in our lives has the possibility of casting a glow across our day. Often it is with someone with whom we never will know their name. A glance. A numinous moment as we cross a street. Through the eyes of a deer that does cross one's yard, one may glimpse the infinity of being. The essence.

The animating presence.

Each of these manifest moments are the experiences of this precious life.

Even the difficult experiences bring awakening and transparency.

I am in gratitude for all that does cross my path.

I am grateful that my daughters, Kimberly Backes and Rebecca Allen are in my life, always adding love and adventure and family! It adds dimensions to my days!

I thank Laura Daen for her luminous role as a muse and friend, always inspiring one to create what brings joy.

I thank Pam Myers for always being there to hear about my next passage.

I thank Violet Roberta for her impassioned and fiery words about the book cover, even before the book was published. The words...touching!

I thank Aaron Rose for the aesthetic support and the attunements in landing this creation of both book and the cover.

I thank all the ones who come for Soul Sessions and Retreats who allow me to 'hold space' for their Beingness that Already Is. It is much the same as sitting empty and opening for a passage in a book to come.

I am in gratitude for all of Nature for always and ever reflecting to me the Animating Presence in all of Life. Even in the tiniest of insects.

I am in deep appreciation for the following technical support, which I so needed!

Art Scanning by Swanson Images, Bob Swanson, Weed, California

Design and layout and editing by Aaron Rose, Mount Shasta, California

Photography by Laura Daen

Introduction

The following passages that have come to me are a passage from one state of consciousness to another higher level of Consciousness. They provide an opening to slip through. Awaiting is a higher dimension and harmony that already is.

I have included the first four paragraphs of the second passage, *What is the Animating Presence?*, as the introduction to this book.

> *What is the animating presence? Where does one find it? How does one access it? Endless questions may come, making it seem so complex, so far away, so impossible.*
>
> *What if the answers were simple? So very simple. So simple that the reasoning, rational approach just ignores and skips over them. Ever trained in complexities is the intellect, not knowing information from consciousness, not knowing human sense of knowledge from Awareness, direct knowing.*
>
> *And what if access to the animating presence was simple? What if you could open to it and allow its animating influence anytime, anywhere?*
>
> *And what if you were the only thing holding you back? What if you were the only blockage? What if your desires are standing in your way? What if your controls, manipulations are standing in your way? What if your simple human beliefs are standing in your way? What if your beliefs in right and wrong and fear are the obstacles? What if your belief in the sense of separation from this inner presence is your barricade?*

What if your belief in two powers, the One Power and "another" power, is your barricade?
What if your belief in evil augmented this sense of twoness (two powers)?

This book is a simple reminder that as we open to this inner presence…an animating presence…alone…that "passages in life" do come to all of us. In many forms. Insights, hunches, intuitions, aha moments, discernment, vision, impulses, creativity. The mystery arriving both within and without.

This animating presence flows through us, as our very being, as we allow.

We ourselves may open to this flow of the Creative One within. And we may behold and witness the animation in our lives.

*Most passages come in the night or predawn when I am very empty. Others come while I am driving on a solitary journey and am still.

Preface

"Open to the exaltation of the animating presence
that you already are.
It will never lead astray.
Trust your Self.
Trust the Withinness.

In opening to this animating presence as our true identity
and being, we do open to see the emerging new culture.
And we do see this animating presence in everyone,
everything and everyplace.

Our lives simply become the bringers of the new frequencies.

Even bringers of the new values
and the ever new forms of balance lived.
Bringers of beauty.

Together…we are the birthers of the new Earth culture.
Together…we behold the Changeless One come
as endless change.
Together…we experience the rapture of the numinous Earth."

True Progress: The Feminine Values

Progress! What is progress? Who defines progress in society? Who defines progress in your own life? And is what has been defined as progress sometimes regression? And perhaps even regret?

The progress as promulgated by industrial society is based on economic growth. It is based on quantity. It is based on goods. More and more goods.

Products. Producing. These have become the goals and gods of our society, all in the name of progress.

We have accepted quantity instead of quality of both products and life. The feminine values have been hidden away. Demeaned. Essence has long been ignored. As has beauty. And caring. Not only caring for each other, as a hive of bees for its individual bees, but caring for the Earth. All the Earth. Her plants, her animals and her minerals. Even her air, her soil and her water.

This greed for things and money has been rampant. It has strangled much of the essence of life. Greed is insatiable. It is destructive. It destroys the delicate balance of a culture and of the Earth.

What is it we, as individuals, can do to rise to a higher frequency of living? How is it that this balance will return? What is our role?

We can devote to our Oneness with the light of Consciousness. That will open the stream of living Consciousness in one's own life. That will open the well of beauty. That will open the clarity of direction. That will open the world of purity.

And simplicity. Simplicity shall be known. And giving.

Taking shall fall away.

Loving will return. And caring.

Illness shall fall away.

Progress shall have a new measure.

Progress shall be measured by the presence of invisible values arriving in lives that are abundant.

Crimes shall fall away.

Hunger shall ever fall away.

And suicides. They shall end.

Stealing will steal away into oblivion.

Progress shall be seen in purity.

The water shall be pure.
And the air.
Even the soil.
The food.

The pollutants that gag purity shall fall away.

Pollutants shall not numb and blind society of its impending consequences. Call it doom. Call it whatever you would like. The imbalance is the same. The imbalance caused by pollutants in all levels of living is killing and destroying life. It is maiming life. It is causing suffering.

And still it is ignored.
The ignoring (ignorance) shall end.
It shall fall away.

To say that we have polluted our minds, our lives, our Earth is not a judgment. It is a description. It is an awareness.

And we can make another choice.
And we can make it now.

False progress via pollution can stop now.
How can it stop, one does ask?

The people can stop it by what they consume. What the people consume is what they support. Be supportive of the essence value that is purity.

This shift from progress creating pollution and destruction of the Earth to progress creating purity of culture is the shift of imbalanced living to the universal law of balance in action.

We must question everything that we buy, starting with ideas. Does the idea enhance all of life? Does the idea bring Beauty? Does the idea add more love and caring and quality to the world? Does the idea contribute to wholeness?

We, the people, are the drivers of the vehicle of progress. We are in charge. As we purchase, consume, use and support.

Let us ponder progress. Progress is a progression. Where are we going? What are we creating?

In the classic, *Pilgrim's Progress,* we see another form of progress. Spiritual progress. We too can turn within and hear the soul speak. The soul has an exalted life. That is our life, should we choose.

In the Soul life, conflict falls away. War shall cease. War economies across the globe shall be no more.

There are ones that say this is a complex matter. It is ever complex only for those who stay ever in the human mind. Ever dissecting. Ever analyzing. Ever trying and struggling to get more.

In the purity of the heart, life arrives as simplicity. Progress is no longer accepted as power, money and more and more. Indeed, that shall be viewed as a harbinger of horror of past history. It shall be viewed as primitive, cruel. As a way to plunder the Earth. As a way to bring pain.

In this purity of the heart lay new visions, new choices and a new way of being and doing. The doing arises from the Being. And balance, it is there.

Life on planet Earth ensues as an illumined kaleidoscopic hologram in full synchronic order, in full exaltation.

Smiles are everywhere.

Humanity is invited.
The invitation has always been there.
Waiting to be known…

*Added note: Sometimes people choose organic food simply because they heard it is better for the body. No pesticides. No herbicides. And on. Far bigger than this, we choose organic because it creates pure soil, pure water, pure air for our bodies and the bodies of the plants and animals. And for the Earth herself. It is for that that we choose. We are choosing not just for our individual self; we are choosing for the One that we are.

Written at 6 a.m. on June 13, 2012, in Mount Shasta

What is the Animating Presence?

What is the animating presence? Where does one find it? How does one access it? Endless questions can come, making it seem so complex, so far away, so impossible.

What if the answers were simple? So very simple. So simple that the reasoning, rational approach just ignores and skips over it. Ever trained in complexities is the intellect, not knowing information from Consciousness, not knowing human sense of knowledge from Awareness, direct knowing.

And what if access to the animating presence was simple? What if you could open to it and allow its influence anytime, anywhere?

And what if you were the only thing holding you back?
What if you were the only blockage?
What if your desires are standing in your way?
What if your controls, manipulations are standing in your way?
What if your simple human beliefs are standing in your way?
What if your belief in right and wrong are obstacles?
What if your belief in the sense of separation from this inner presence is the barricade?
What if your belief in two powers, the One Power and "another" power, is the barricade?
What if your belief in evil augmented this sense of twoness (two powers)?

That is a lot of what ifs! And to move through them, we can open to know the truth. We can let go of learned or pretended position, that mimics what we have heard, read or reasoned.

How do we let go? It is easy. We open to know the truth.

We just give up. Open. Be receptive. Be empty. Listen within. Feel with the soul.

The left brain way of teaching has been to parrot, memorize, mimic. It has been rote and disciplined. It has been in a rigid box and most often leaves no room for questions, intuitions, insights and endless ahas.

Note: I was a high school and college English instructor and wrote curriculum in the summers. I was also a coordinator and liaison in public educational TV, so I understand well the box that is the so-called educational system. The true meaning of the word education is to draw out that which is within. That which is already within. When children have true educators, we shall see joy across the lands. For those children will be free to expose their authentic selves, their true natures. Their animating presence!

This animating presence is within. This animating presence is accessed through receptivity (the feminine principle of man and woman).

So what is this animating presence? And why would one want to go within to access it, to feel it? To realize it? This "what is it" will answer those questions:

This animating presence is the Unspeakable. It has no definition.
It is the Silence that brings the sounds.
It is the Stillness that brings motion.
It is the Emptiness that is the fullness.
It is the placeless place that is timeless and spaceless.
It is the Changeless One that is the change.
It is the Undivided One come as the seeming two of yin and yang in all of nature.
It is the wordless and the nameless, though we give it many names.

It is Invisible. Formless even. Yet it appears in form.
It is is pure Consciousness. I Am Awareness.

Now do you know what the animating presence is? No, of course not. You may have only heard definitions that have been given for eons. In the eons of definitions, why is not the world filled with spiritual teachers and illumined ones? Because memorization is not the It! Is not the animating presence. The "letter of the word" is not the It. These teachings may increase our desire to know direct and realize the It. And studies may resume through the ages.

But until the desire arises to know, to realize this It, this animating presence directly, then there may not be penetrating and piercing of the mental definitions. The arousal and arising of this desire supersedes the attention of the external world. And then the "letter of the word" is known as the "spirit of the word."

Those who have experienced and had illuminations and revelations of the reality that the world is within may then become wayshowers, that is, showers of the Way!

The Way is simple. Children know. Fear and all of its offspring of doubt, worry, anxiety, misery and suffering and endless stresses are not The Way. This fear and its offsprings are warnings. They are signals. They are cues. They are our innate system that shows that we are walking down a dark dead end road full of thorns and compounding problems. They are part of our navigation device.

If we acknowledge we are moving and living in the belief in fear, we can change our direction. So allow the arrival of fear, in all its many guises and costumes, to be your navigational system giving you the red light. Pay attention.

Give up. Surrender. How? Open. Be receptive. Listen within. Feel the animating presence of your Being. Allow.

There is a powerful word. Surrender. We see it in sacred teachings. Just surrender...we are told. Over and over again. As if there was a magic surrender button or if we could just go to a surrender workshop enough times. And still the surrender eludes millions, seen in the warring of imbalanced homes, states, nations and on.

How is surrender accomplished? Is it an achievement? Or perhaps there are as many means of surrender as there are people?

What each of us can share is our experience. That story. We are always hearing...drop the story. It is my experience that the story can be as a parable. It can create the portal or opening in consciousness that gives the deeper understanding of surrender.

Some of my story: When the restlessness and suffering of life became so great and I could find no way out, the word surrender (give up) arose in my mind. I tried many techniques for surrender over the years and finally I just shifted my seemingly human awareness to Awareness. The I Am Awareness. The cosmic consciousness. I just let go. I did not do this by trying.

I opened, became receptive, listened and felt the Withinness. I felt with my Soul faculties. I began to feel the animating presence.

The animating presence became my greatest friend. My ally. The beloved. That One that is the animating presence in me, you, everyone, everything and everyplace. It is the All.

As we open to it, feel it, allow it, we then have acknowledged it. We must acknowledge it, welcome it, for it to animate easily through us and as us. As our very being. Once we have acknowledged it and felt the gratitude, it can begin to grow.

It is then that we hear with no ears and see with no eyes.
It is then that we have glimpses into the seeming mystery.

Acknowledgment brings glimpses. Some small. Some into the
Vastness.

O the petals of Mind do unfurl like a dancer in the night,
unveiling unspeakable beauty. Essence and purity uncaptured
by the mind.

Love that knows no depth or width and cannot find a person.
Love as Consciousness. It knows no limits and is itself.

When this comes upon us in the "surrender," which is the
receptive heart and mind, it is seen as absurd to look for
love. Love just is. And we allow. We allow love and wisdom
to be revealed through us. Giving love a body. Giving love
an expression. If we are open, we cannot help it. Mind and
manifestation are one. We allow.

It has only seemed troublesome when the human beliefs come
into play.

How is it that we allow this animating presence, without the
ravages and miseries of the human beliefs?

How is it that we stay in the Oneness Consciousness rather
than the belief in the sense of separation that we have named
duality? That we call good and evil?

What would it be like, dear friends, to live in a world with
the realization of The One Power, rather than the belief in
the black hats and white hats, the never-ending battle of
polarities? What would it be like to live in a world that knows
no opposition?

O, I am told it is impossible. Study the six thousand year
human history. See the endless wars, terror, horrors and

insanity. That belief in impossible is the doorway into those realities. It is the very realm one has chosen to explore and experience. Hell realms for eons.

O, we have been told reality is in the outer, the seeming external and material world. If we believe that, we are caught and trapped in our own belief. And we shall demonstrate it whether we love it or hate it.

It is only when we open to the "world within," which is the true animating presence, that change begins to come. We begin to experience harmony, supply, the perfect people in our lives. Joy, even rapture, it is known.

There may be some bumps or seeming problems and challenges here or there. But they are short-lived. We know how to live in another state of consciousness, a frequency that is ecstasy. And we open to that.

We open. We are receptive. We listen inwardly. We feel the frequency.

There was mention earlier of feeling with the Soul Faculty. How does one do that? How does one feel with the Soul? Through desire. Desire is the key that takes one deeper. Desire is what allows us to know with expanded awareness, rather than with the brain. Desire of this deeper nature opens the door to grace.

Here, that which we thought was personal is known as the Impersonal. The Impersonal One. Pure Consciousness.

What if someone shared with you that they had experienced very deeply the Impersonal One? The I Am Awareness. What if they then said that there are no personal ones? There are no persons. There are no separate human minds. There is only Consciousness expressing, manifesting AS this seemingly physical plane of existence. As what we call persons.

These people have been called saints, mystics, insane and hallucinatory. The entire gamet. It all depends who you share it with. Another mystic. A psychiatrist who has not opened. A child.

If it is told to the wrong person, you are a sinner.
If it is told to the right person, you are a saint.

We are neither, I say. We are pure Consciousness, both being and expressing.

So back to some words that bear repeating. Open. Be receptive. Be aware of breath. Listen. Feel. Feel the animating presence. Be aware. Be aware of Emptiness itself. Be aware of Awareness.

And now. Identify with this animating presence. Over and over identify with this animating presence. Identify with it, that no longer do you suffer from mistaken identity in this so-called physical world of materiality. No longer do you identify with status, career, mission, partner, husband, child, car, house, body, nation, even the seemingly human mind and thoughts and on. No longer do these things define your days and define your nights.

Yes. Identify with this animating presence. It is your very self. It is your Soul Self. Your Light self. Your Love self. Your infinite self. The Self of Selves. The true self. The authentic self. The One Self. The One. There is no other. The illumined one. And there is joy!

Who taught us to identify with the external world? Or even our beliefs and thinking minds? Why did we go down this road? How did we get so caught up in these complexities that have led us astray from The Way?

One could receive endless PhDs in those fascinations and intrigues, for life after life. In time.

Or one may open into the Timeless Realm of the Real and realize this I Am Consciousness, this animating presence.

Written in 2011 in Mount Shasta, California

*In the winter of 1997-98, in a meditation home in Crestone, Colorado, overlooking the San Louis Valley, I had a vivid lucid dream about aerial viewing the seeming unfoldment on the planet Earth. I was shown how to see it through a child's "dot to dot" creation. And as we move from dot to dot, the big picture is ever seen more clearly. Each of us is part of the dot to dot creation and of our collective awakening. Ever are we seeing the "big picture" more clearly. Ever do we individually shine light, expanding Consciousness. Such beauty. And experienced is the animating presence! The One.

Holders of Unborn Dreams

Friends, we are here! Awa Tey Ewa Tey. Now is the Time.

We are not talking about shifts in the future. We are in the shift. It is a River of Convergence. The water of Life flows strong, heading toward the quantum torus. Heading toward the realization of Unity Consciousness available to all who choose it.

It is time that together we choose harmony with nature.
It is time that together we choose the universal law of balance in all of nature.
It is time that we respect all of nature.
It is time that together we choose to awaken to and experience our oneness with all of nature.
That we can feel the sounds of nature…the owls and on…
That we can feel the light emanations of the flowering buds in the spring…and on…
It is time.
That time is upon us.
It is time that together we choose purity.
We are not choosing it for our personal self.
Friends, let us remember the Impersonal Self.
The One.
We are One.
There is no other.

We must choose purity for water, air, soil and food. For the animals and the plants.
We must support that…for all of nature…the kingdoms and the elements…
We must choose for the good of the whole…or we shall perish.
That is not a doomsday prophecy.

That is ever a clear statement of choosing our individual and collective destination...as the One.

Never in all of time has there been a moment when the Universal Appeal thunders into all the ears that great change is upon us.

Are we listening? Are we seeing? The human body and the Earth body have symptoms. These are powerful alarms, signals, warnings that we are going the wrong way.

The local and worldwide warning system must be honored and heeded. They are signals. We must learn to read the signals. And like a flock of birds in the sky, we must turn together to make the change.

All have a sacred part. All here have a precious role in the change. All are instruments of the One, should they care to choose.

Economics as we have known it was never the game of Life. It has ever been a game of might over right. It has ever been a choice of greed of the personal self over the good of the Whole, the Oneness.

We are not talking about political ideologies.
We are not talking about political systems and the endless isms.
We are talking about The People.
We are talking about an uprising.
We are talking about an uprising from within the people.
This uprising emanates from the heart and the soul of the people.
It is the coming forth of the One as the Many.

That is the time that is upon us.
It is a time that emanates from the Timeless Realm.

Such laughter and joy is upon us should we open to feel.
Such limitless horizons for creation lie before us.
Such episodic adventures of untold wonders.

How would I know?
I carry stories of sight from other realms.
I come from a future that awaits us in the now.
I am a holder of unborn dreams.
I contain the same Divine Memory as All.
And I do come to tell.

What is the guardian of the threshold?
Your very heart.
Your very heart does have the answers.
You must know your heart.

Your heart is ever a silent field.
Your heart is ever an emptiness that is a fullness.
Your heart is ever a vast intelligence.
And a pool of infinite love.
And it is yours.

You are that love.
You are that one to give the love a body.
You are the one to create the market place of love.
You are the one that shall strip the systems of greed by
outpourings of new forms.

We are the birthers of new forms.
We are the birthers of infinite forms of love.

Rapture shall be known across the lands and across the seas.
Boundaries shall cease. And wars.

Ever shall the world home sing to the stars and to the very stones.

Such is before us and within us…even now!

Thursday, March 17, 2011 (St. Patrick's Day of the wearing of
the green), received in the wake of Japan earthquake, tsunami
and nuclear disaster

The Garden: a parable

a modern parable, a parable for now

The Garden never went anywhere.
The garden is inside of us.
It resides there as truth.
It resides there as beauty.
It resides there as love…
as the peace that already is.
It is ancient.
It travels into our awareness from original awareness.

In the 50s even, some of the seeds of the garden were sown.
Few noticed. Again in the 60s and 70s, more were sown.
The farmers were called hippies. They were sneered at and
ridiculed. Dismissed as dirty, with no goals.

Those seeds took root. They were seeds of truth. They began
to take root and grow. More were planted in the 80s and 90s.
Tiny plants. Hardly seen by the collective. Even in 2000 and
on were they planted, fed and watered. And they grew.

Also the weeds did grow. The weeds of untruth grew tall. And
taller. Ever dwarfing the truth. Ever dwarfing the premise.
Everywhere false premises became the pretend foundation of
the garden. A foundation can never be a lie. That is the seed of
its own destruction.

The weeds took over the garden. Most of the people thought
the weeds were the garden.

The true seedlings were called weeds. Often laughed at. And
those who planted them were chided and mocked.

The weeds of untruth began to overtake the garden. The

weeds proliferated with ugly distorted roots. They became formidable. Even frightening.

All in the garden felt somehow wrong. No one could figure out what was wrong. The weeds were prospering, but the garden was failing. What was wrong?

A few courageous ones began in the 60s to pull a weed of untruth here and there. The weeds exposed revealed the polluted thinking and the polluted world.

Time continued. More and more brave souls pulled weeds and exposed the weeds here and there. Some were frightened. They said that if everyone pulls weeds the gardeners who planted them would be angry. Others were so busy helping them to plant more weeds that they would not take notice. Immense denial became the thwarted dance of the day and then days.

The untruth gardeners hired some "hired hands" to help in the garden. Their job was to make sure that the weeds were not pulled. And make sure that no more truth seedlings were planted. Thus the garden became policed.

The ones who began to pull the weeds and show the distorted roots realized that by showing the roots, the false premise, in the light of day, that it could not grow anymore. And the garden would change. The Real Garden could finally grow.

O millions of seeds have been planted by now. Ever soon it shall be billions.

These seeds are planted in humanity's heart.
They are illumined.
They are awaiting.
They are the template of humanity's collective truth.

O the garden...
It is beautiful...

29

It can be seen ever within your heart.
It is planted in your heart.
Never can it be destroyed.

Now is the time to see it glowing on this plane of existence.
And growing.

Now is the time to bring what has been called fantasy and
fiction to bear on this plane of existence. To bear fruit. This
garden is not a fantasy. It cannot any longer be relegated to
some far away movie or pretend dream with no realization.

The most humble of positions on this fair Earth.
A gardener.
Become a gardener.
Today…become a gardener.

Plant seeds, beyond a dim hope for the future.
Plant seeds of illumined knowing.
Plant seeds of truth.
Everywhere.

And spend time in this seemingly personal garden plucking
out the weeds. Big ones. Small ones.

O I tell you my friends.
The weeds must be exposed.
They must see the light of day.
They shall wither, dry and be the compost of what you think
of as tomorrow.

Show others the weeds. Show them so that they too can
identify the lies and distortions. The giant weeds are harder
to pull. It may take creativity and it may take more than one
weeder. But it can be done.

O dear friends, do you see how much fertile compost is
coming? It is being prepared even now.

Teach those still planting seeds of destruction and those guarding and policing the weeds what they are doing.

Teach by planting the seeds of love.
Teach by infiltrating with plants of peace.

Do not forget how important weeding is.
Do not forget how important it is to be aware of weeds of untruth.
In denial…shall they continue to grow.

Let us together…assist the gardeners of truth and the weeders of lies.
Let us together…watch the garden grow.
Let us together…celebrate this transition time of exposing and pulling the weeds.
Let us together…celebrate the growing compost pile of new free energies available from the arising phoenix.
Let us realize…we are one.
We are…the undivided one…

This simple parable arose at pre-dawn just after an uncomfortable dream.

My own sometimes dismal past in a few man/woman relationships became the teacher in the dream garden.

Dream:

I am with a man I recognize. He has just left me, again, for another woman. I become aware that this happens to me and the other women in the dream because no one will name the problem. No one will name the lies. In the dream, I realized I desired to expose the seeming problem (the weed).

In the company of this man and the women gathered in a large bathtub (dream style), I exposed the entire problem and the lies (Aries style).

31

What happened then was amazing. I could feel the mental/psychic movement of everyone dealing with the hidden, unspoken finally voiced and spoken. The forbidden. The forbidden was now seen. A weed picked. It would not be enacted again. The lie was done. Finished.

I awaken.
It is dawn.
I am lying in bed and this garden parable begins to waft into my sleepy awareness.

I can clearly see the power of admitting what is not working. Exposing it. When it is exposed, it has no more grounding. No source of food, water. No nourishment. Demise is known.

It was never the truth. Truth is Real. This miscreation that has no basis in truth may fall away. That is its "unreality" exposed. And light may show its face and features!

Let us no more call the gardeners of truth "conspiracy theorists." They are angels bringing the light of truth. Provide a flashlight. Even a floodlight. Or better, just awaken and let your own light of Being, Light of Consciousness, flood the garden.

The Light of Source does grow the garden. This garden will maintain and sustain itself. It has a foundation of and in truth of Being. It flowers.

And together, with this ground of Being, we may explore the stars, the mists and beyond.

And crisis is no more.

*There has been an insane reversal of thinking in the last 50 years. It is often legal to lie and often illegal to tell the truth. This reversal is finally exposed that the crazy-making of a few may bask in the light of Source!

All blessings to the tellers of truth. Do not relegate them to the name whistleblowers or even protesters. They are blessed among people. Heroic. Noble. Warriors of Truth! Tellers of Truth. That light of truth may shine undistorted and unperverted in this precious garden of Earth. A landing template of Light!

And crisis is no more.

Friday, December 9, 2011
Writing started from a dream around 5 a.m.

The Invitation is Sent

What if?

What if what you are looking for in speakers and lecturers
cannot be found there?
What if what you are looking for in books and movies cannot
be found there?
What if what you are looking for cannot be found in words?
Or in thoughts or beliefs and on.

Just what if?

The world loves magic and Merlins and potions and elixirs
even. Movies and books attest to that.

What if elixir existed?
What if it is available, even now?
And what if it is free?
And you can access it anytime, anyplace.

Would you want it then?
Would you want it if it were not far away?
A mystery?
Unreachable?
Would you want it then?
When no longer do you need to dream of it, pray for it, fight
and have flights of fantasy for it?

What if finding it was upon you? Now.
Would you recognize it?
Does it need to be packaged, marketed, promoted a certain way?
Does it need to come via a certain organization or institution?
Need it be adorned?
Need it be named?
Need it have an outer tool?

Must you make a long odyssey or spiritual pilgrimage to find it?
Must it come through a person?
What are your beliefs?
What are your limitations?
Self-created and self-imposed.

What, I say, would it take for you to get more simple?
What would it take for you to open to the indigenous mind?
What would it take for you to be receptive?

What, I say, would it take for you to be empty?
What would it take to say yes?
What would it take to know you are in command?

I tell you. You have these answers.

When yes Resounds, the questions and the answers, they shall fall away.

Found, my friends, is the elixir. It is an essence. An essence of the infinite. It has many names or none. This essence is a sacred carrier. It is the love we have looked for. It is the wisdom we have sought through the eons and long ages. It is our supply. It appears in our world as the perfect forms, conditions, situations, food, people, and on…that are perfect in our journey.

The Impersonal Journey appearing as the seemingly personal.
It is the Formless Essence as form.
The Invisible made visible.
It appears as our very lives. Life.

And always, this intelligence, this love is here. Revelations, intuition, impulses, ahas, inner feelings, gut feelings, co-incidents, etc…all directing our life, our show.

Outer programs, beliefs, boxes, cages of the mind do fall away.

The inner being is recognized. Enlisted.

This essence of the One emanates from you. Others are ensconced in its embrace.

Belief in lack falls away. Belief in doubt does leave. And suffering. Fear and all its offspring disappear in the Light of Knowing. The Light of Being.

It would seem that I try to make it simple. In utter simplicity, sometimes in destitution, it is recognized. Then acknowledged. Then realized.

This elixir is your very Being.
This elixir is Inexhaustible Supply.
This elixir is awaiting.
It awaits.
It awaits the fearless ones who ponder wonder.
It awaits the fearless ones who ponder freedom…and, yes, ponder your origins beyond the stars in the sky and the thoughts in the head.

How does one share that which is prior to words?
How does one realize that which you Already Are?
How does one share the mornings beyond magic?

Days move into nights.
And nights into days.
And we study the great mystery.
Volumes are consumed and the mind is fed.
The soul sits waiting.
The chalice of elixir is full.
The invitation is sent.
Come.

December 1, 2011, written about 3:30 p.m.
Mount Shasta, California

I AM Awareness of 1981

I have spoken many times of my 1981 awareness that happened over a nine hour period as an I AM Awareness. Still I am assimilating and integrating it.

Let me start this way. I have had lucid dreams where my two eyes function just like the zoom lens of a camera. I can look very close up or at a distance. My eyes just zoom in or out as needed for the situation. And I seem to be right there or far away. It happens with ease.

Those dream experiences gave me the idea of doing a "zoom lens" yoga exercise for my eyes. I stand outside or at a window. I look far away and feel my eyes with great sensitivity. Then slowly I bring in my range of vision to something, such as grass or a flower, that is very close to me. As I am bringing the vision from broad and distant to close, I am feeling the lenses of my eyes. Then I do it in reverse. From close to far. And I repeat that numerous times. It is such a relaxation and joy for the eyes.

Now, I will use the zoom lens analogy for the awareness in consciousness that I am going to describe.

It is 1981 and it is 9 p.m. I am meditating with a friend. After a while, the friend goes to bed. I continue to meditate until 6 a.m. Nine hours. It is actually more like an immense expansion into the so-called Vastness that is natural and comfortable.

Remember now the zoom lens analogy. Only this time, the seeing is inward with inner vision, but it is still like a zoom lens.

I am sitting with my eyes closed. In the Stillness. All of a sudden, I hear a dog bark. I can hear as Mary with my physical ears. I can also hear inwardly with inner hearing. Then I hear a car. The same thing happens, only it feels even more expanded. Then Mount Shasta and area is both outside of me and inside of me. Then the state, the nation and the Earth. Simultaneously it is outside of me and yet inside of me. Clearly the world is inside of me. The world is within.

Everything continues to expand, like a zoom lens. Everything is both external and internal simultaneously. I become aware of the cosmos. Galaxies. Star Systems. The sense of separation is dissolving.

As this zoom lens effect continues, I, that I call Mary, begin to disappear. I, Mary, no longer exist in the so-called normal way. A person named Mary is no longer part of the experience. Via the zoom lens experience, I am aware of Consciousness. Simply Consciousness. I am only aware of three words once I am only aware of Consciousness. They float in, yet not as words, but as awareness. They are: I AM Awareness.

This Vast Awareness is the One Awareness. It is the Source Awareness that has multiplied into the many that we, everything and everyplace, are.

There is no Mary being Aware of I Am Awareness. There is only Consciousness itself, Undivided, yet paradoxically manifest as the many.

Everyone, everything, everyplace is Consciousness. There is no material universe. There are no personal minds. There is one divine mind, pure Consciousness. And it is good. It is Immeasurable Joy itself. No words shall ever capture or define.

So back again to the chair at 9 p.m., meditating. I enter the Timeless, dimensionless as Consciousness. It happens smoothly like a vast journey of Consciousness, but really it is not a journey, for there is the "Revelation of Consciousness"

Alone! And that includes all, here now. The seemingly personal does not exist. The Impersonal Alone appears.

Consciousness, the Undivided and Unmanifest, does appear!

The zoom lens analogy simply serves to elucidate the Unmanifest as the manifest. And to elucidate the One as the Many.

The entire experience serves to shift my long time identity with body, form and thoughts to the eternal identity. I Am Identity. From the seemingly personal to the Impersonal.

The next chapter of Life was to learn how to navigate easily upon this precious planet Earth dressed in biology, without losing the true identity. The challenge has been to both be fully embodied and fully identified as the One, simultaneously.

As more and more get it individually, the collective self-governing will naturally and organically continue to reveal itself as the One Life, in balance, harmony, purity and sacred rhythm.

Labor Day, September 5, 2011

*I was driving to McCloud, California lower waterfalls. Just before I arrived, a wolf crossed the highway in front of me. I had been thinking of going to the lower falls to write about the experience of 1981 as the One Mind, I Am Awareness. And I continued to flash on the analogy of the zoom lens of a camera.

Education...and the face of radiant joy

There is much that will have to change in our educational system. It is built upon memorization mainly and mental prowess. That is a system of rote, repeating and parroting. Copying, really. Individual expressions of the infinite turned into copies. Like carbon copies. Or clones. Left is a dry and brittle intellectualism.

The shift in consciousness that must take place in the school system is the realization of where Intelligence comes from. Within. Intelligence cannot be trained. It is innate. It is what one is. It is the wisdom, the consciousness of the universe.

The children must be taught how to open and how to listen within. This openness is a receptivity. It is the feminine principle of the cosmos that has been so long ignored in the western civilizations.

Listening within has been too often relegated to some religious attribute that maybe one does on Sunday.

Listening within is a way of life. It is the avenue through which wisdom is found as the heart of one's very own self.

Listening within needs to be the core of the educational system.

Listening within and knowing directs our own navigational device.

The listening within is finding the teacher within, the wisdom within, the direct knowing within. It is how the Wholeness Consciousness is found. It is the way in which Pure Awareness is accessed. This innate wisdom is the simple voice of wisdom, just awaiting notice. Available, ever, at one's turning to the Great Withinness.

This Great Withinness is our riches. It is the substance of creation. And we may let it flow as our very Life.

This Great Withinness is Intelligence, Wisdom. It is the education of the "so-called" future. It is beginning now through each one that turns within to the heart that already knows.

We each need look no further than ourself. That self is the One Self.

And, yes, we do need the practical education. That is obvious. Like the young animals that learn how to act or what to eat from watching the mother. Yes, the ABCs help us communicate and create. They are practical tools.

Yet it is the Essence that knows what to create. It is that which brings the beauty, caring, order and balance. Vision. Sanity even. It is that which never would be a builder of wars, nor be the cause of suffering and pain to people or animals or even to the Earth herself.

Battling about which direction to move with civilization is to miss the point. Any battling is to miss the point. The Withinness knows no battle. There is no opposition.

The Withinness pours forth a richness that ever adds to the fabric of culture, that ever contributes joy and laughter. And dancing even. Ever does it sing of our Oneness.

Ever does battle fall into oblivion.
Ever does hostility disappear.

And ever does joy share her radiant face.

Monday, September 5, 2011, written at 4 a.m. on Labor Day

What grace shall break the seal?

Yea! I am here. I am here in a voice you may hear. I do hearken unto you. I do call. Always I do call. Are you listening? Listening turns into realization. Realize that which you listen to. It is Mind. Not human mind. There is no human mind. There are beliefs. Beliefs block Mind, while Emptiness calls. And why call me Emptiness, when I am the Fullness? Such is the way of words. O how they do strangle and suffocate the realization. O how they mask the freedom, that which has never left.

You do love the words…I call you. I speak to you. I am here. You do love to say…I long for you God. I search for you and do seek. I thirst for you. And hunger even. You do love that sense of separation. You do love that I am here and you are there. You do love the…I am returning. I am going home. The prodigal enhanced ever by movies, novels, poems and soul-searching songs. Never-ending tears.

It is the belief in self seeking Self. Ever do you love dressing in the costumes on the stage of duality. On a stage that exists only in the imagination. O how you love to imagine and fantasize and weave yarns. Make-believe.

O how you work to keep the chasm wide between your sense of me and thou. Subtle are the languagings that keep the "tension" of seeming separation going. The sense of lost soul instead of I. The Impersonal I. I Am.

How many meditations in the ages and eons have been conducted to finally find God within? Freedom. And how many realized beings have you met? Millions? Thousands? Hundreds?

What has kept this secret of realization from the people?
What blasphemy has sealed the fate of believers of duality?
What grace shall break the seal?

August 26, 2011, Mount Shasta, California

The Brilliance of a Thousand Suns

Friends. Dear Ones. Precious Souls. Awaken. Do awaken.

Learn to stay aware and alert to all the ways needed to keep and brighten your Light. To do that, be aware of that which traps, dims or steals your Light.

I am not speaking to give you more beliefs. Nor even to advise or counsel. If you desire to awaken, you will Awaken. The teaching, the guidance, the endless direct knowing's shall ensue from within. They shall pour forth from within your heart and soul. They shall illumine you. Enlighten you. They shall uplift you from the world of duplicity. Duplicating ever beliefs that keep you in shackles and chains. That keep you harnessed to falsehoods. Whatever you believe shall rule your life. And you shall create your own suffering born of ignorance.

Ignorance is an ignoring. Ignoring is clearly a statement of "I don't want to know." It is a form of denial. Ask to know. Ask to discern between entertaining information and Knowledge. Reveal to your Self that direct knowing is wisdom, an elevated Intelligence.

This innate Intelligence is that which informs you.
It is that which imparts to you.
It is radiant. Luminous.
It brightens your way.

This Intelligence may seem or appear to one's reasoning mind to be moving blindly. The opposite is true. The ever thinking mind that has not glimpsed from a higher and bigger vision and picture is both limited and engaged at some level with a belief in separation and fear.

Clear sight and clear vision have no questions. Nor do they have problems. There is simply Life Lived by this Intelligence, this wisdom awaiting our notice. Clearly, it is at the point the Emptiness is known as the Fullness.

Such paradox is ours. And beyond. Life is. Isness Calls. We can awaken to this call of Light, the Light of Knowing.

Freedom reveals Herself.
She reigns.
She stands tall.
She is yourself.
And She shines.

Dimness does lose existence.
Dimness no longer holds one captive.
Dimness leaves the stage.

Brilliance enters.
The brilliance of a thousand suns.
Shadows cease.
Self soars.
Laughter takes flight across the lands and the seas.

April 17, 2011, written on I-5, driving from Orange, California to Mount Shasta, California, on full moon and one day after my birthday

The Animating Presence in All of Nature

This animating presence of Light is not something that we use. We open and are receptive. We experience and feel. We realize. And It uses us. It lives as our very Being.

We have been doing it backwards. Humanity made the mistake of using It. Using It to control and manipulate our lives and others' lives. And we have created global imbalance at many levels that simply continues to compound the catastrophes and disasters. Even endless disorders. And none need happen. O how humble humanity may be with this realization. And none need happen.

As we open to this animating presence, human beliefs do surface, ready to fall away into the Vastness, ever to be recycled Energy in our lives. Ever to increase our awareness of the Inexhaustible. That inexhaustible supply of chi, energy, animating presence.

Never do we need be upset when these human beliefs in a world of seeming separation surface. These beliefs may arise in thought as judgments, opinions, interpretations, translations, perceptions. Allow them to surface. And these beliefs are just that, thoughts. We need not suppress them. We need not deny them. We need not engage them. Or analyze them. Or even indulge them. Just be aware. Be the watcher, the observer. The monitor even. Behold. Allow them to fall away. As if they never were.

We live in a thought wave, light wave universe. Thoughts and pictures are everywhere. Good ones. Bad ones. We need not engage. Simply notice.

What is key here is to notice from this awareness of animating presence. It is outside of humanity's maelstrom of discordant thoughts and endless battles about right and wrong.

This animating presence is love Itself. It is Intelligence Itself. It is the very substance of all creation that arrives and appears as our lives. Your life. My life. All lives that are open to It.

We open to being a transparency for this animating presence.

And how do the thoughts fall away? They are simply thoughts. With no indulgence or reaction, they can fall away. We are the ones who have identified with them. We are the ones who then had fear. We are the ones who fueled the thoughts. We ourselves have been the givers of power. The givers of power to a belief in two powers. And we created victims and victimhood.

There is no blame or shame here. There is only change. That change is the opening to the animating presence. That opening will allow ones to live in the realm of the real. The make-believe world of two powers has ever only been an individual and then a collective nightmare. It is time. Awa Tey Ewa Tey. Now is the time. Now is the Time to awaken from the collective nightmare of hellish realms that we either created, allowed or in some way participated in.

Thespians. Theatre. From human theatre to sacred theatre. That is the shift in this awakening. Fully awake to the animating presence. Sacred theatre arises now as a way of life and being. We are our own director. We are Self-directed. Self-governed. The actor in us shows up fully identified as the animating presence of light.

It is important to know that it can shock some. Stun them even. And that is not the intention. It is ever only everyone arriving as the One.

When we are listening and feeling inwardly, instead of empathing outwardly, there may be ones who would like to "guide," even control our lives. To act as if they know where we should be. Even, when, what and with whom. Should we not follow our own direct, inner knowing of our lives, it will be easy to go astray from what you know to be true for your life. Resist ever the temptation to follow another's advice and suggestions, unless it rings true for you. Resist ever the temptation to please others or use following them as a way to be accepted or liked.

Open to the rapture of following the knowing of the One Self, the animating presence of the One Light that you are. It will never lead astray. Trust your Self. Trust the Withinness.

Be willing to let go of ones who do not rejoice in your inner knowing, your intuition, your insights. Your direction. Be willing to let go of ones who do not invite you to speak your truth. To live your truth. To follow your heart and soul.

Should you stay and debate and argue and discuss with such ones, you will possibly open to doubt. Doubting yourself, your insights, your very life.

Life is not a debate. Life is truth lived. Life is the animating presence of Light. This light is the light of Consciousness. It is the sacred carrier of the love and wisdom, the yin and yang of creation. It is the very substance of creation, appearing as our lives.

O how humanity suffers. So busy demonstrating material world.

And now we shift. Let us demonstrate the animating presence of God. Let us see then how our lives do shift and change. Without trying, efforting. Without struggle and stress. Without the fear.

After six thousand years of a history of pushing, shoving like a bully in the schoolyard, do we shift.

We open now to the animating presence. We realize both the masculine and the feminine aspect of our being.

The Dance of the One appears as our life. The yin and yang of our own being. Within. Without.

How does it reveal itself in the without? In all of nature? The animating presence in all of nature.

There are many ways we can open to this experience of the animating presence in all of nature. Many ways may be revealed to any of us. Stay alert. Stay alert and be aware of It everywhere. It is everywhere present.

One way of opening to the animating presence is to be guided from within to a place one loves in nature. Attune to and identify with the presence within. (One may find one's own way to do that or read *The Holy Sight* or listen to *Journey of Consciousness.*) In that growing attunement, become aware of this presence within your being, as everywhere present. Omnipresent.

Say you are sitting at the shore of a lake. You are deeply feeling the inner presence. Start with your eyes closed. As this feeling of Life, that is the animating presence, grows, allow yourself to feel it deeply. Feel it in your heart and in every part of your body. As it deepens, be in the gratitude. That appreciation and thankfulness may increase what you are feeling. The gratitude may be expressed in whatever way you want. In the silence, even with no words, may be potent. Sincerity is a key. And open as the sense of this universal energy may grow, expand, deepen. This gratitude is the law of supply, increase, multiplication, abundance.

When you are ready, open your eyes slowly, still feeling this inner animating presence. Softly look out at the natural scene around you, staying fully aware of the presence within. As you look out at a cloud, moving in the sky, be aware of the animating presence, moving it. Feel it. As you look at a bird, in flight, become aware of the animating presence living in the bird. AS the bird. Feel it. Notice a ripple upon the lake from a fish or even a tiny surface insect. Again be aware of the animating presence of ALL life. Feel it.

Each time you feel this animating presence, be grateful. In your own way. Feel the presence grow and expand.

Next become aware of a slight breeze blowing across the wild flowers. Again be aware of the animating presence. This is the One Presence. The Only Presence. It animates all of nature. Including us.

And be aware of a tree or an herb growing nearby. You may not see motion. And still you may attune to this animating presence that is Invisible. And formless even. And you may feel it. And be aware that It is appearing as form. The Formless One as form. And feel this Formless One. Such ecstasies do arrive as we attune to this animating presence that appears as our Life, as all lives.

We need not know biology, geography, names or labels to do this. The less information that clutters our minds, the easier it is to experience the awareness of the animating presence in all of nature. In sacred inner Silence.

Probably most everyone loves nature and being in her presence. Yet not everyone realizes what is being experienced. Essence. It is the One Life. And there is no other.

We may experience this every place we go in nature. The awareness of our interconnectedness and interrelatedness grows.

The human sense of other will begin to dissolve for humanity, while paradoxically being so aware of unique expressions of the One Presence. The One appearing as the Many.

This may all seem way too simple. The human thinking mind would like it to be more difficult, so that it can compete and compare with others. Or, even, is there a way to add substance, so it can be packaged, promoted and marketed. And so that progress and evolution may continue to be measured as economic progress. Quantity instead of quality and value and beauty. Impossible to measure the Immeasurable One.

With the arrival of the awareness and acknowledgment and gratitude of the animating presence, the spirit, is the simultaneous awareness of the masculine/feminine in balance and equality worldwide. In this, the world will not stay the same. Structures promoting imbalance may no longer survive. They are in their death throes even now. Only those forms that emanate balance and are for the good of the whole may flourish and grow.

The climate is changing. In this new frequency of love, a climate of the new culture, the old shall pass away.

In opening to the animating presence as our being and that in all of nature, we do open to the emerging new culture. Our lives simply become the bringers of the new frequencies. Even bringers of the new values and the ever new forms. Bringers of beauty. Together we are the birthers of the new forms.

In meditation, many times, when I open to this animating presence, this Christ presence, my inner vision does open and revealed is the Realm of the Real. Heaven on Earth. The new Earth culture.

Over and over I was uplifted into Changing Woman Realm. Revealed was a world of ecstasies. The world as we have known it disappeared. Revealed was the illumined Earth. Revealed was euphoria of being. Revealed was the ever changing landscape and forms. Revealed was the Changeless One come as change.

Changing Woman was revealed as an original archetype of being. She is illumined and is the Birther of New Forms. She is Shapeshifter. Changing Woman feels the animating presence in everyone, everything and everyplace. Changing Woman-SHE becomes the very sea, the flowers that be, the sand upon the ground. She realizes SHE is the One. And you are SHE.

This, my friends, is a little of the gift that will be given as the world comes into yin/yang balance. All the talks of justice, fairness, equality, caring, nourishing, truth-telling are the talk of the "effects" of that balance. With the balance (love/wisdom) manifest, all else shall follow. Because there is "no other," the conflicts shall depart. Imparted are the wisdoms borne of balance.

Let us...together...invite Changing Woman!
Let us...together...allow the new humanity!
Let us...together...open to the animating presence in all of nature.
Let us...together...experience the rapture of the illumined Earth...

Written in 2011

Ever shall she teach us how to soar...

I am at the waterfalls. It is beautiful. There are enclaves of families and friends. Women are sitting serving food to the standing men and youth.

In the new Earth, the women must serve more than meals. The food must be values which constitute spiritual food. Until these values are served, women will be in servitude to the continued old ways and old paradigms. Until women wake up, break the patterns, actions will continue as usual. Conflict, wars, bombs, fighting. Same actions of rape and pillage in one form or another. Again and again.

Woman, awake, may change all of this. Woman, awake, may serve the awareness of a world of love and caring. Woman has the power to break the ties of painful old forms.

The world awaits woman to journey deeper into her heart. Disclosed shall be a world where harmony dances. The challenges that arise shall be of finding and birthing the ever new forms of Being.

Ever shall woman nourish her family and the world family. Ever shall she show up as the birther of new forms. Ever shall she point the way to realms and dimensions never imagined by a mind limited to a material universe, even a mental one.

Ever shall she teach us how to soar.

Ever does she cry in consternation when a wing does break.

Ever is she patient until there is flight.

Never shall the world return to the dismal times.

It is done when woman says it is done.
Woman may turn this page in humanity's history.
The heart's torch has never dimmed...
It has awaited our notice...
And the Light...it is bright...

Saturday, July 10, 2010 (grand cross day)
Written at Lower Falls in McCloud, California

The Unlimited One

Finite activity or Infinite Activity. Which of these is manifesting in your life?

The mental realm of consciousness is material and ever is it limited. And ever will it bring frustration, anxiety and perplexity. Those can bloom into anger, rage and even hatred. The material world continues to look outside itself to go beyond limitation. And never shall it find the Unlimited in the pockets of darkness, competition and so-called economic progress set forth by political agendas.

The Unlimited always is accessed by those connected to the Source, wherein lies Abundance.

Masses of humanity have reached a place where it is now enlivening to learn what it means to plummet. Ever is humanity looking for new adventures in the sea, the air, on and into the earth, even to the far reaches of space. And all the time that eons of exploring do continue, the satisfaction eludes those who search. The world is within. This plummet within is the ultimate adventure. It is the most daring of all adventures. For it has no competition, no end, no destination, no timelines. There is no booty or plunder. There are no awards and degrees. There are no titles and status.

The treasure found in this plummet is the Limitless. It beckons us. It forever calls our name. It awaits prior to beliefs and speaks in the language of the soul. To each, its communication is different.

This plummet is a free fall. This Limitless One does maintain one's life. That which manifests is the mystical as the practical. The well-known word made flesh.

In this plummet, we are out of control in the mental way of understanding. Now it is…that Divine Control is experienced.

Here there are increasing intuitions and glimpses of how the Oneness is unfolding. No one and no thing is independent of this unfolding. We are the One manifest as the many.

Humanity will begin to reach unprecedented awareness of unique differences. No longer will differences be called weird, odd, strange, unaccepted. Differences in races, religions, cultures and individuals will be welcomed, respected and deeply honored. It will be known that the uniqueness is part of the Oneness in its purity of expression. It will be known that the fetters and blinders of belief and concept have been swept away. It will be known that this is the synapse point between that which is finite, limited sense and that which is the plunge into the Limitless.

Hospitals and prisons everywhere will transform into centers for this plummet. This adventure into the Oneness. Ones everywhere will begin to see this rarified world of the Limitless. They will cry for and beg for escape from the limited mental entrapments of the sense of separation. Epic fear and its adrenalin rush.

When this free fall plummet is found, the world will finally witness epic change. This will be the change that has in its wake the sense of wholeness that all have been seeking. All are seeking the One. As the deepening takes place, we are observing ones everywhere leaving the cages of conformity.

Everywhere we see the cosmic deck of the fool appearing. The fool arises all around us. This appearance frightens and delights. It frightens those who are bound with rules that no longer serve this cosmic transformation of the ages. And the appearance of the fool delights those who await this sacred enactment of the One, knowing it is what will call others out into the Play.

Those in the plummet shall begin to reap the cosmic harvest of the Infinite Activity through them. They shall both traverse the stars and serve as wayshowers to the naysayers that grasp the straws of finite activity that brings endless dissatisfaction and closed doors.

The epic adventure has arrived.
We are in the free fall.
And freedom is what we are.

July 4, 2010, written in Mount Shasta, California

A New Culture Exists...
housed by The Third Kind

The Inquisition. The Inquisition never ended. It simply changes form. Throughout history it morphs into the shape of the times. Burned at the stake. Drowned. Beheaded. Shot. Tortured. Raped. Mutilated. Herbalists decimated. Healers prosecuted. Run out of town. Given false charges. Nothing has changed except the calendar dates and the forms.

Now we have a CIA and on...that can murder and create trumped up charges. The imbalance of the master/slave role is not new. Quite ancient. It has been with us as a symptom of the sickness of humanity, of the imbalance, of the false belief in separation that has been perpetrated worldwide. We pretend that we are many when we are One. One alone.

The slaves, enraged, scream and shout for freedom. Freedom from. They battle and fight. They create unions and associations. Greatly do they charge into this miscreation, like don Quixote and the windmills. Fiercely do they yell their battle cries, writing yet another chapter in the epic movie of humanity's belief in opposition. Two. Freedom from. Freedom from the made-up other. Lost are the subtle nuances that unveil the harmony. The One. Almost lost are the signs of yet another world, pulsing with an Indescribable Something. That Something eludes those who slumber. And those who ignore. And those who deny.

And there is the third kind. Ever do they live and dwell outside the insanity. Ever are they the watchers. The monitors. Ever do they act when there is an Opening. Ever do they pronounce another way. Ever do they stand at the door of freedom beckoning those with eyes to see and ears that bend to hear.

This third kind is a growing and unstoppable mass migration. As seasonal swans do they find their way into a grand garden that is a new Consciousness. They are as sentinels at that door of Consciousness. It is not a migration to a place. It is a migration to a state. That state of Consciousness is within and is ever the One.

And the Inquisition turns to dust, forgotten in memory, fertilizer for the new world garden.

Freedom rings in the heart of humanity. Are we listening?

The current Inquisition lies hidden, scarcely noticeable until now, cleverly disguised as some corporations, governments, pharmaceuticals, heart associations and on. Some religions. Even some banks. Wall Street. They are all long arms extending from the original Inquisition. It is like Halloween in reverse. Instead of innocent people dressing as monsters, the monsters are well dressed as humanitarians, the altruists of the world, the very saviors. A well planned and staged reversal. And the collective has bought it in the marketplace of beliefs. Agreement was made. The media has made a clean sweep.

And now…freedom rings…in the ears…and many are listening.

A new Culture exists, housed by the third kind.

Monday, May 3, 2010, written while driving to Silicon Valley

The One Realized

The collective consciousness of humanity is being invited to be aware of and realize Oneness Consciousness, that is the illumined Mind. Light...the sweetest carrier of love and wisdom.

It is as we realize this Consciousness that we realize the interconnectedness, the interrelatedness of all. And finally the realization that we are One. Not just with each other, but with all of Nature everywhere. Minerals, plants, animals, devas. The earth, air, water, and fire elements. In that realization, one will be in holy relationship with everyone and everything. In that, will the universal Law of Balance, which is the law of nature and the law of love, be lived.

This inviolate and inexorable Law of Balance is about equal giving and regiving in all relationships. We must open our hearts and actually feel the love that we are and realize it is the same love that all are and all is. In that recognition, direct Knowing will be experienced. The oneness realized. Heart and mind, earth and sky, yin and yang realized as one. Opposites but no opposition.

Then it is that we live the mystical as the practical. One might then ask, "How may I have this realization, this initiation?" The answer is in your heart. Go there. Feel the love. Listen. Trust. Allow.

You will begin to break the spell of humanity's epic affair with the drama of duality in a "seeming separation" from the One, allowing false beliefs to dominate, creating fear and its endless offspring of disease, suffering, pain and wars.

Let us now "feel" this great presence (by whatever name, be it spiritual, traditional, scientific, religious, generic, quantum, etc.)

in our heart and our Being, as it is everywhere present. It is the wordless, nameless One. Sacred vision, holy sight for all will become the norm in the new Earth.

Awa Tey Ewa Tey
Now is the Time

October 2009

An Invitation to Holy Relationships

Humanity is awakening out of a long sleep in duality, a sense of separation from Spirit, God. The Light that we are. That we may end this slumbering, that is a collective fear and suffering borne of that sense of separation, is a certainty.

We may shift our awareness to the Consciousness that we already are, beneath the wall of beliefs. We may breathe in the Light that is everywhere present and "feel" it. It is who we are. We may then "feel" it in our heart and being as the light body within. A template of Infinity. The world is within. Awaken to that and our outer world…it changes. From the Changeless One comes the ever-changing world of form. The dance of the One.

Once we come into this holy sight (sacred vision) for ourselves, we can begin to have this holy sight for everyone, everyplace and all of Nature.

We see the truth of Being…
We see the wholeness…that already is…
We see the true identity of all…
We feel this holy presence of Light…as everywhere present…
We experience holy relationships with everyone and everything…
We experience and remember the One that we are…
And we enter a new world…
It is here…now…

Awa Tey Ewa Tey
Now is the Time

October 2009

What is Awakening?

What is awakening? What really is this freedom, this liberation? This precious grace? Who is awakening? What is awakening?

Really, there is only the awakened state, only we have it blurred or blocked with beliefs. Those beliefs create an immediate sense of separation. That sense of separation immediately sets up a sense of fear. And fear births endless offsprings, of endless names…anger, anguish, suffering, pain, doubt, insecurity, lack, poverty, hate, human love with motives and on and on down the ages.

And those beliefs have been built into civilizations and religions and sometimes traditions for eons. They serve those who want to control. They serve the people not at all.

There is not really even a state. It is Pure Consciousness. Pure I Am Awareness. That is Spirit, God, etc. It is our very Self. There is only One Consciousness. There is no other. There is no God and……! Everything, everyone and everyplace is It. There is no Divine Mind and human mind. Only Divine Mind. And that Mind and manifestation are One. With no separation. Mind and Matter…one. The world is within.

We even keep ourselves from It by intrigue, curiosity, intellectual prowess, indulging, analyzing and on. We pretend It is outside of us. So ever we have hide and seek.

We find It in the Inner Silence. It is a vast pervading stillness. Emptiness. Nothingness. It is the Fullness. And we know that It is everywhere, everyone and everything. Presence of All. Omnipresence.

All these are only words unless we have a direct experience, direct knowing. Most people have had at least a glimpse of this. And everything seems to flow. What we want is Flow all the time. We want life that is Life. We want flow that is Flow.

This Beingness is the River of True Life. We can't buy it, sell it. We can't think our way to it. Or do a workshop to it. Reading about it is not even it. Although all those things might prepare the heart or the soil of the thinking mind to receive it or we might drop more beliefs that do not serve.

We cannot chase it, pursue it, achieve it, become it. We cannot transform or trans-anything into it. We are It. We are Already It. We are that I Am that I Am. How could one become that which One already Is? This Isness is the It. Even desiring It can be subtle. For how can we desire that which we Already Are? That sets up a sense of lack and "don't have consciousness" again. Very subtle.

It is an opening, a relaxing into, an acceptance of What Is. What Already Is.

You can study all of this in the ancient teachings or contemporary ones. Or you can open to It in the Stillness that is the pervasive Presence. Breathe It. Feel It. Listen to It. Allow It. Identify with this Unity, Union with Good. I and the Father are One Identity. It is the Illumination that is the Light of Presence, of Being.

Know this Essence to be the very Self, including your very self. It is the true identity of all. This is what has been seemingly lost. We look in the external world of seeming forms and find it not.

This Essence is the substance of all creation, the substance of all form. It will sustain and maintain Itself. It is Self-fulfilling. It is Supply. It is the bringer of joy and beauty. It is the joy and beauty Itself. And laughter of the Gods.

This Presence reveals All as the Everything. In that, it is realized, there is no duality. There has never been a duality. There has ever only been a belief in duality. There is not God and...! There is only One. Oneness. The One knows no opposition. The One is in the Dance of the One. And the dance of the One as the Many. There are opposites, but they are not in opposition, conflict, battle and war.

Why is this awakening to what and who one really is so difficult? There is no one to wake up. In the awakening, it is seen that there is only Consciousness as the All. Any belief systems would not want that. That would be its demise. A sure and certain death. Marketing and packaging in the marketplace would not be needed.

One can see the "seeming" problem here.

It is the One Self Realization that is desired here! Claim that! A new culture emerges.

Fall of 2009
A friend asked me the question, What is Awakening?
Some time after that came this article as a response.

There is Spirit Alone
There is no Spirit (God) and...

In our solitary withinness, we make the claim of Oneness. We feel it. We experience it. We are it. Then we open our eyes and there is another and another and another. It seems.

We end up having the Inner world and another seeming outer world. We end up embracing Reality and a seeming reality. We end up believing in good and evil. We end up in separation. It is a seeming separation, for separation does not exist. It is a thought of separation. It is a belief in separation. And the appearance is so.

Some people will fight this Awareness. They will refute it. They will argue about it. And debate. And the fact remains. There is One. One Reality. One Existence. One World. One Consciousness.

O how the gods must laugh at our creations. O how futile are these thoughts and beliefs of separation.

In our sanctuaries we pray for peace. In the seeming outer world, we prey on wars at every level. We are in our own self-created conflict and know it not.

This consciousness of conflict is an inner world of conflict externalizing as an outer world of conflict.

How do we reconcile these two worlds? They cannot be reconciled. For the beliefs of separation are not real. They have never been real. They will never be real.

Friends, I hear you say, "This is hard to believe." Or even, "I don't believe that." For those of you who say "I don't believe that," I admonish you to put it in your neutral file and keep an open

66

mind. You might consider something like, "Spirit, please reveal the truth; show me." Go ahead and read like a Kansas license plate. You might be surprised. And for those who say, "That is hard to believe," I say that you have in your very words, in your very languaging and in your very thought structure created your own barrier to knowing. Consider carefully your words. Consider opening to the Silence and sitting in the Unknown. Sit in the Unknown to open to the Known. Open to Direct Knowing. You are then embracing an expansion of Awareness. I have worked with many across the globe. Some of them actually say, "I don't want to know." That is great. They are honest. At least they finally know that they don't know because it is their choice.

Jesus said, "I and the Father are One." That simple line was the scientific fact expressed. There is no separation. What appeared to be healings was merely Jesus seeing that…All and God are One. He literally saw Perfection, Wholeness, Completeness. There is no other. We could spend eternity trying to heal sick minds, bodies and worlds. In that we have claimed our belief in separation, imperfection. We have not I Am that I Am, but I am two. And duality comes crashing in all about us as a world in conflict.

There seem to be two worlds we are living in. One is exalted; the other is fear, and its offspring of pain, disease, anger, misery. Ever endless forms of suffering. A belief in separation is a world of suffering.

There is Spirit Alone. All One. The Consciousness, Awareness, Realization of That is a radiant world of opposites with no opposition. It is an illumined world of appreciation and thanksgiving as the One World stands revealed.

November 16, 2008
Driving on I-5 from Mount Shasta to San Francisco in the a.m.

True Investment

Early predawn, I woke up remembering a dream I was having. People were all around in numerous small groups. They were speaking about losing their investments. They were very upset with losing their money. I seemed to have a role, a reason to be there, but I was silent and just observing. And I was then waking up. As I looked back into the dream, I found myself asking what the dream meant to me. I felt as if I was in the dream to educate the people gathered about True Investment. I sat up in bed and wrote those two words. True Investment.

....

What is a True Investment? We invest in what we put our attention upon. No matter what the subject or object. Whether we like it or don't like it. Whether we are giving or receiving. Whether we are happy or sad.

We feed and fuel and add to that which our awareness is upon. We create it and fan the flames of its existence. For that moment, it is what we are living for. We are "trying on" that experience. Whether we are conscious of it or not. By making it our present moment, it becomes our seeming future moments.

When people work hard and put their dollar earnings into an investment, they usually do it as a way to save and/or multiply their earnings. Generally they invest in things that are popular in the culture, so the earnings will be larger.

How many are looking at that investment as a "creator of society?" How many are deeply looking at the long range results and effects of that investment? How many are asking if this investment creates a better world? How many are asking if this investment is good for The Whole? How many are asking if this investment is good for the earth, the air, the water, the plants and the animals? How many understand that The Whole is more than the people?

To invest is to support! Our investments are our life's energy. It is that which we say yes to. It is that which we agree to birth into the world. It is our heaven or our hell.

We are responsible for our investments. What we buy, consume, use, we support.

The subject of investment gets very subtle. Say there is a war and you support your troops. It looks as though you are being loving, caring and filled with compassion. If we look deeper, we can see that supporting troops supports the entire moral and financial mechanism of war. They cannot be neatly compartmentalized. They cannot be separated. And if we were truly heartfelt, wouldn't we support, not only our troops, but all troops, and the women, children, babies and elders that are swallowed into the war games? Where does war between men separate from the society? To invest in war at any level is to invest in war. Our attention is our participation.

So back to our subject of True Investment. We each will have to investigate what is actually meant by true investment. If we have a true investment, we will have to dig deeper than the superficial idea of personal savings. What is personal when we are One?

A true investment brings value, purpose and meaning to The Whole of Life. A true investment supports qualities, not just quantities. A true investment contributes to the beauty and purity everywhere. A true investment adds joy and well-being to the world at large.

Ask this day…what do you want to invest in?
Ask this day…what do you want to support?
Ask this day…where you can contribute?
Ask this day…what does your perfect world look like?
Ask this day…how you may create that perfect world?

How can each of us contribute to and create a perfect world?

True Investment is investing in the consciousness, the awareness of Perfection. Some will disagree with this, argue with this and even start debates about this.

The idea of Perfection sounds to many like some religious diatribe or some fanatical fantasy. Something to be shunned and squelched even. It is something that is impossible they say, so best to cast the next movie with ever more diabolic figures of destruction. It covers and hides all dreams of Perfection. It ever puts ones into a trance. And numb are our lives.

In the meantime, the awareness of Perfection waits in the wings to be noticed, to take flight as your imagination, to soar and then land upon this precious Earth.

The awareness of Perfection opens the limited and conditioned mind of reason into a Mind of all possibilities.

No longer can beliefs thwart dreams.
No longer can they block inspirations.
No longer can they bury and silence visions of the heart.

Our True Investment is an investing in the dream that lies waiting in our heart. And there is but One Heart, One world. One. And, together, we are that One.

Together…let us make that True Investment.
Together…let us feel that one pulsing heartbeat of people, Earth, existence everywhere.
Together…let us feel the love of that investment.

What…together…we earn from that investment is riches beyond compare. A new world ordered by the universal heartbeat pulses as our very lives.

A new culture…emerges.

And vigilance is called for. We must notice if we are investing in prophecies of any kind. Doom and gloom, Armaggedons, disasters and disorder of any type. Just by gazing into these scenes of hell, we are investing. We are intrigued and fascinated and entertained even. We indulge and engage at such subtle levels, watching all the details. We are habituated into and accustomed to reactions. We live in that constant adrenaline flow, thinking that is what makes us feel alive.

That is a paltry and empty substitute for the feelings of Aliveness. We can invest in a new picture. We can stop investing our time in perpetuation of the pictures of hell realms. Some are even addicted to fear, that familiar emotion of being scared. Shock flowing through every cell. Our need is almost to be electrocuted with these hideous images. Consumed by them. Such insanity…to invest in and pretend we can thrive on images of the imagined hell realms of separation, destructiveness and divisiveness. Emancipation ever eludes us.

Unity calls.
Invest in our Oneness.
Invest in that.
Freedom rings…

Sunday, November 2, 2008, written at predawn

The Heart of the World

Hey, what's the deal? We have people across America and the world doing jobs they hate. They wish for the weekend. They can't wait for Friday. They drink after work to unwind. They take jobs they don't like for health benefits. They take jobs they don't like for good pensions. They take jobs they don't like for early retirements.

Why are people living lives dreaming of evenings, weekends and retirement? And would we do that if we were living our Dream? What made serving one another in love turn from the nobility of Creativity and Work to work and drudgery and even misery?

What has gone awry in our homes, education and our governments? Whose agenda are we living instead of our very own Self, our Heart? Why is it this way? Why aren't we asking these questions? Why don't we stop long enough to find the answers? Why do we sleep on? Snore even. And walk and even live in our sleep.

It is time for the people of the world to ask themSelves new questions. Deep penetrating questions. Questions from the heart.

Why am I really doing this job? Why am I looking into the future for my security? Why do I believe safe, secure and stable is outside of me? External to me? Who believes that? Who taught that? Who conditioned that? And why?

Why was I taught that education was information poured into me? Why was I taught that everyone else should make my decisions? Why was I not taught to think? Why was I not taught the true meaning of education? Educo, a Latin root word for education means to lead or to draw forth what is already within.

Just being told the true meaning of the word education would have changed my life. Just listening within would have changed my life. Just following my heart's desire and dream would have changed my life and billions of lives.

The world. The world would not look like this. The world would not be full of wars, torture and famines. The world would not be oppressed, depressed, impressed and compressed with social and political agendas and control and endless devious manipulations.

Wake up people! The American dream and the world dream. It is in your heart. It is in all hearts. In hearts everywhere is the truth. Your truth, my truth. The truth in the heart. It awaits the internal expression, that external pressures are no more. It awaits our knowing.

No one can do this for us. We ourselves must stop and go within. We ourselves must ask the right questions.

A new culture emerges and it is filled with joy. It is filled with joy Unspeakable. There is no outer key. Money won't buy our way in or status or the right job or knowing the right person. Control will not get us in or fast talk or any talk.

Our own heart will direct us. We have the answer. Our very thoughts, words and actions are the answer. They must ensue from the heart, from the very Soul.

It can seem scary. It can seem lonely. That is only because no one taught us that in our heart we are connected. We are One. We are related. In our heart, connections begin to happen; our energy starts to flow. Dams built in the mind do burst.

We are the very Energy that flows. We are that Life Force. We are Life itself. It is Living us. It is not us living life. We are the very Life. The One Life.

Joy surges. We feel love flowing. We love others. We love life.

What are we waiting for? Nobody is going to make us do this. In fact, we might even face resistance. It can come even from those we love. We might be told we are crazy. Fools even.

We must go deeper. Where does "freedom ring?" Freedom is not something the world gives to us. Freedom is something we are. We Already are freedom. We must exercise it. We must practice it. We must let it flow from in our hearts. Freedom is in your heart. Your Consciousness that is the very Self.

Let me tell the story of a job I held many years ago. I was the master tutor at a junior college. I was hired to help students with English and Math. I could easily see how miserable they were when they arrived to be tutored. I must now confess that I did not tutor. I did not follow the job description. I followed my heart. I followed the intuition that revealed another job description. I trusted it. I followed it. Results came.

As each student came, I would ask what the problem was. After listening to them tell things, such as the tutoring department showed them all the career magazines and the statistics, they began to draw a very strange picture. These students were being guided into filling "slots" in our industrial and technological world. They were being herded into slots to keep the economy going. It was all about money, all about profit. No one was being asked what they enjoyed, what they liked, what they were naturally and instinctively drawn and attracted to.

No wonder they could not learn. No wonder they had blocks. No wonder they seemed to need tutors. No wonder no one "saw" them.

Once each person told me what their problem was, I looked across the table at them and I asked, "What is your Dream?"

Many responses came from that simple question. Sometimes tears would come. Some would look at me astonished. Some would say, "No one has ever asked me that!"

No one has EVER asked me that? What? What kind of world are we living in that these questions of the heart are not being asked? These most important questions of a Lifetime. This is the question that can make or destroy the Life flowing in you, through you, around you and as you!

Friends, this is your Life! Life must flow. A stifled Life is a crippled life.

Once Life is flowing, you may bring stares, resentments, jealousies, even ones giving advice to turn back, to change, to conform. Once life is flowing, you may scare people and seem reckless and unreasonable and illogical.

Such wild freedom and untainted joy can bring fear to those not yet in their hearts.

So back to the tutoring. It was my experience that when people are pointed to their heart that tutoring is not needed. The block is gone. In truth, the mental block was rather like the soul's protection. It was the warning. It was the heart's directive letting us know we are on the wrong path. We are leading someone else's life. We are merely filling a slot to fulfill someone else's dream.

Where are we going here? It is simple. Humanity does not need ideologies and external directives flung at it. In fact, it needs quite the contrary.

We have left the Heart of the World. Our hearts beat together as the one heart. Our hearts know what we want to do, be, give. How can we give our true gifts, our true talents if we have not let them flow?

Imagine! What will the world look like when everyone everywhere is living from the heart? What will the world look like when this Self-governing is finally in place? What will it look like? We all need to do our part of this Whole.

In that, your life becomes an inspiration. Your life becomes a model. As an example, others will follow your lead. They will turn away from the dark, murky, vague fear that keeps them in restraint.

So I ask the question now, that I asked many students years ago, "What is your Dream? Not your dream, but your Dream. There is a great distinction."

If your answer is "I don't know," then ask to Know. Find the Silence, the Stillness in your Heart. Ask to Know. Open to Know. Allow direct Knowing. Follow hints, intuitions, impulses. Listen to your Self. Let the crowd do its own thing. If you need time to be solitary, trust it. Honor it! Do it. You will not regret what Awareness, what Consciousness, can pour from in the heart.

Feel the life with the heart. Feeling is the inner key. Feel the flow that is your Life. Newly found feelings and impulses may emerge. Allow them. Heed them. Take action.

This Life flowing though millions and even billions is creating a new culture, a new Earth.

And joy…it is ours.

The answer is in the heart. The answer to these questions is in your heart. It has always been there. It is simple.

After you have done this and your Life is JOY, people will notice. Then one person by one person, the new culture of the heart will appear.

And I tell you. It is here.
It is Already here.
Only the heart can show you the way.

October 16, 2008, written at 1 a.m.

Protectors of Women

Where are the protectors of woman? Where are the men? Why are women in nations worldwide still harmed, abused, maimed by men? Why are women, at any age, bought and sold into slavery, prostitution and even marriages that are not real? Why are women called helpmates? Why does this imbalance exist?

Some women have participated by allowing governments, religions, traditions make of them subjects, often less than the animals. But woman have tried to give their gifts through the ages. Inquisitions happen every day in the lives of millions of women.

While it is true that women are awakening and finally making more and more shifts to bring the balance to the world home, that is not the point that I now make.

I ask now the men of the world, why aren't you protecting the women? You have a big responsibility in this arena, all down through the last 6000 years. Where have you been? What have you been doing? You may need to dig deep into your DNA and pull out the roots of this tremendous imbalance. You may need to open to your heart and soul. You may need to leave the desire to be superior. You may need to leave your fear of woman. You may need to leave your desire to control and manipulate. You may need to leave the logic and linear thinking of the left brain.

How will this be done?

First it is important to note that resistance to this universal and inviolate Law of Balance will cause further pain, anguish and suffering.

To surrender and allow it to happen is the easiest way. Put the attention in the heart and soul. Allow the Presence found there to embody. Feel it.

Allow the fast emerging culture of balance to be revealed as your very life. Help other men find the dwelling place within that brings only balance in its wake.

Millions of women already feel and see what is happening worldwide. Through women, the world will finally have a Mother. Through women, the world will finally have protection. Through women, Beauty will find its rightful space on Life's stage.

Men…everywhere…protect the women.

Men, never shall you be happy making woman unequal. Her inequality is your inequality.

Men, never shall you be happy making women the spoils, the booty of endless needless wars of barbarism created by the minds of insanity and imbalance.

Men…everywhere…protect the women.

June 9, 2008, driving to Silicon Valley from Mount Shasta

Wholeness Is:
There is Nothing to Heal

There is nothing to heal.

Wholeness Is. There is nothing, no one and no place to heal.
What? I hear minds begin to ask. Nothing to heal.
No. Nothing.

Find that place in Consciousness where Wholeness Is.
Where Wholeness resides. Where Wholeness has always been
and always will be. It abides.

It is Consciousness. With a capital C. It is Mind with a
capital M. One Mind. Ever only One Mind.
That is the All of Existence.

All else is belief. Just things arising from belief.
Conceptual notions entertained, indulged, engaged.
O how fascination creates endless travels and travails of
illusion. Curiosity…it killed more than a cat, dear friends.

Ever must our attention be on this Awareness of Wholeness.
Ever must we be aware that only has there ever been a
Spiritual universe and a Spiritual Existence, though the
opposite seems so.

Tricked we are as we see the railroad tracks come together
on the horizon.

Tricked are our senses as we see the lake, a mirage,
on the desert floor or the road beneath our feet.

And tricked we are as we buy the belief in human good
and evil and that which needs to be healed.

Ever do we miss the sweet ecstasy of being that lives pulsing in our heart and the pulsing in the universe.

Ever…ever…do we miss the true manna that awaits our notice.

Ever…it awaits.

Countless travels we create and travails that need not be.

While ever…It awaits…
Wholeness…It awaits…
It awaits our seeing…
It awaits our feeling…
It awaits our realization…
And grace does fill all space…

May 27, 2007, driving to Los Angeles, California

It Is Quiet Time:
A Child's Exploration
of the Heart

How many hundreds upon hundreds of times did I find myself saying to my daughters in the early evenings of their growing up that...ok now...it is quiet time? I repeated the words "it is quiet time" endlessly for years. After a busy day, I saw initially that it was I who desperately needed quiet time. I saw that I needed to find the stillness of my being in a restful atmosphere like a sanctuary where space from others was deeply valued. Later I saw that even my children were deeply nurtured from this quiet time in the evenings. They were creative and peaceful in this quiet time. Respect and honoring of others was created in this quiet time.

....

The value of quiet time in the life of a child is beyond measure. The quiet that ever abides in the heart of each child must be tapped, felt and known.

The finding of the quiet time is found in the stillness of the timeless born ever in the heart. Here resides ever a place without distractions.

Too often the children of today are bombarded with television shows, commercials, constant interaction, constant entertainment, intellectual/brain stimulation, food and drink stimulation, medical/pharmaceutical stimulation, endless transporting, movies, animation and outer oriented music.

Wise is the parent who can educate and inspire the child about the value of "quiet time."

Wise is the parent or educator who can lead the child to "quiet time" where lives essence, the true identity.

Wise is the one who leads the child into valuing "quiet time."

Many are the points of departure for the child who has "quiet time." This is the child that will understand and live in balance. This is the child that will know from where comes flashes of inspiration. This is the child that will understand the center of its being. This child will begin to perceive the fulcrum of the universe. And this is the child that knows from where joy arises and laughter and the love in their hearts.

This is the conscious child that shall see beyond platitudes and myths, beyond dogma and never-ending creeds. This is the child that shall hear the voice of revelation borne within the heart, free from distractions of prattle and other thoughts of meaningless manifestation. Grand shall be their distinction between concepts that distract and divine mind thoughts that inspire and animate.

These children shall glow in the recognition of their freedom to express the truth that awaits notice in the heart.

Quiet time is luminous. It awaits radiant as the Sun. It casts no shadows of perplexity nor dark corners of obscurities.

Quiet time for children forever illumines the dark pockets of humanity that would dare to remove freedom or interrupt the universal flow of nature, the very mind of our being. That would dare to scar the Earth and corrupt her elements.

Quiet time for children illumines that which is holy. That which is sacred already. That which is forever Pure.

Does this "quiet time" speak then of impractical dreamers and fanciful imagination and a futile perfection? Does this "quiet time" speak of useless ideals in the ivory tower of make believe? O how the world would try to capture all in the morass of this staggering escapade from Reality into the pockets of a never-ending poverty of consciousness.

Sad is the life of the child who never finds the treasure chest that is the "quiet time of the heart." And desperate is the life of the child beginning the endless pursuit of person, place and thing, the nouns described in language classes around the world.

There is another language that lies waiting in the heart of each child. This is a language of the heart. A language of the inner quiet, a language of luminous perception.

O leaders of the children. Guide the children to this inner classroom. Guide them to this treasure. This is the treasure of their very own selves. And it awaits.

In "quiet time" shall the children recall the remaking of history. In "quiet time" shall the children experience the eternal now. In "quiet time" shall the children dismiss the dismal meanderings of the conceptual world into the horrors and terrors that are fear.

In "quiet time" shall the children discover that the heart has no opposite. There is no Love and…something else. There is only Love. There is not a foreign particle to battle, fight, curse, change or heal. There is nothing there to hurl into the hell realms of duality.

Only Love abides. And Love speaks and jumps for joy.

Here…in "quiet time"…shall the children see a world with no borders and races and prisons.

Here…in "quiet time"…shall the platitudes of unreality fall away…no longer pirating freedom and cloaking truth.

Here…freedom sees.

All of this…my friends…as we voice the offer to the children…
"it is quiet time."

Is quiet time a punishment? A taking away?
My friends…it is a gift. It is the gift of gifts.

It is the time when children see that they are given gifts
from the timeless realm that seem to have no name. It is the
moments of seeming time when children recognize their gifts,
their direction, their movement and flow in the universe.

And "quiet time" is always available. We must teach our
children to value it, to call for it, to create space and time for it.

Together…let us honor the children with "quiet time."

How may we honor the child?

Help the child find the best time and place for this quiet time.

Help the over-stimulated child to find this place. Be creative,
flexible and spontaneous.

Be willing to drop your "outer plans" if it becomes clear the
child needs quiet time.

Be able to identify the child yearning for quiet time, a time to
connect within.

Be ever ready to create the room tone or environment for a
child who needs quiet time.

Understand that the alone time, that is quiet time, gives rise
to the feelings of connectedness and Oneness. It allows for the
awareness of "there is no other."

Understand that in quiet time a great sense of belonging can
arise.

Understand that in quiet time great inspirations can arise in
the child.

Let the child know how much you value quiet time.

Know that quiet time can help the child not have a sense of being trapped in time, space, future, past or concepts of any nature.

Let the child know that…here…in the quiet, the stillness and silence of its own mind…freedom reigns.

How may we lead the child?

Teach the value of quiet time each day.

Let the child know that you need quiet time as well and why.

In each situation, see where and how to create quiet time.

Put on quiet, inner music when it will assist. Or a CD of nature sounds. Or better yet, real nature sounds whenever possible. Go to a brook, a stream or into the sound of the breezes through the trees.

Encourage and entertain this yin way of being…this quiet time. Embrace it with your child. Be aware of excessive activity and intellectual endeavors that may bring stress or imbalance.

Ideas shared by a child during or after quiet time must be listened to in earnest. Sometimes they gather in ideas from far away worlds.

A child may want to do artistic things in quiet time, such as paint or draw. A child may want to quietly sing or play an instrument. Or the child may want to create a story or a poem. Or it might be time spent in a tree house, by a stream, in a field of flowers, on the family couch or under a table covered with a sheet. Each day the possibilities are endless and ever changing.

Great rest comes to the child in quiet time. Sometimes the

child falls asleep, but sometimes the child prefers to get rest in quiet activities.

Allow the child freedom to choose their spot for "quiet time." It must not be treated as a punishment.

The child must also learn to respect and honor the quiet time of all other family members. Later on that will spread into their respect for all in the cultures of the world.

Be willing to move into new directions and expressions as the child begins to explore quiet time.

Encourage the flight of the imagination in quiet time. For here is touched the realm of the real. Here is touched the mystical that can be made practical in their lives. Here is where visionaries and inventors are born. Here is where they see and hear works unseen and unheard by others who quickly folded their wings and entered into a cage.

Take the quality of time to teach the child that in quiet time exists the very substance of creation, that the very manna from heaven falls into consciousness to be given unto the world in endless forms and expressions. Reveal to the child that they can be and do and have anything. Reveal to the child that he/she is the living revelation through quiet time. Reveal to the child that quiet time is a magical time.

Assist the child to perceive that "quiet time," solitary time, is an adventure. That it is an adventure of consciousness!

In all of these ways and more shall the children discover that the greatest wealth is within and that even…the world is within!

And let them know that the giving of this withinness creates that which is regiven to them, i.e. receiving, and that creates a balance in their lives.

Cultivating the awareness of the gifts of quiet time will create a lifelong increase in cosmic consciousness. It will be a contribution to the child and to the collective.

January 18, 2007, driving from L.A. to Mount Shasta

Winds of Change: choosing Purity in an emerging culture

Purity! Is this an old fashioned word that no one wants to hear about OR is this the word of choice in an emerging culture and a way of being and a way of living?

I am entering my ninth day on a trip to Maui over Christmas time. I am greeted with air filled with 90% (I read) genetically modified agriculture, ocean water in which most of the cruise and tour boats dump the human feces about 3 miles off shore, and ground that is polluted with chemicals and pesticides from industrial and genetically modified agriculture. The ground water is also polluted. I read a local article that described the dismay of the young surfer crowd at the water conditions. However, they continue to surf in the contaminated water. I spoke to one local about the air being affected by genetically engineered and chemical agriculture. She said that that was not a problem and that they were fortunate to have the winds that blow it away and clean the air. I reminded this well-meaning person who was very sick that even China coal pollution was now blowing into parts of California via the tradewinds. We are one world and we are connected.

The discussion of purity. Is it old fashioned? Or some might say that I am focusing on the negative.

Friends, I say…it is imperative for our survival and quality of our lives and for all the kingdoms and elements that we choose "purity."

Choose purity. We must choose purity. We choose purity by what we buy, what we support, what we eat. We, the consumers are choosing daily. Purity or pollution. Purity or pollution of air, water, earth and food. We must choose.

Many people are speaking about what we must do for global warming or what we must do to protect the polluted and dying plants and animals and oceans.

Friends, this is a start; caring simply for our own organisms would take care of all the others. In terms we have all heard… our body is our temple. In quantum physics terms…our body is a radiant energy. We are light and we must be the vigilant keepers of that light. Friends, it is we who must keep that light from growing dim or going out. It is up to us.

A new day emerges. And as this new day quietly emerges thousands of tourists are pouring into Maui acting like all is pure as they swim in the ocean and eat from the ocean and from the earth. A new day does come as America ranks itself with some of the sickest people and nations in the world. People will either quit denying the connection between "pure air, water, earth and food" and well-being or they won't. Many would rather choose sickness, disease and even death over admitting the connection. Believing that the purity of earth, air, water and food supply does not matter…is just that. A belief.

Beliefs are not truth. They are just beliefs. They are thoughts that pollute the field of awareness. Beliefs dim consciousness of truth.

Until we become empty, taking no thought (or belief), we cannot be a pure transparency for the Divine Mind.

Pure thought of the Divine One Mind can then be the order of the days and of the nights.

Never-ending plights of human condition shall end as if they never were.

Then we shall no longer cover up the pollution, pretending it is not there.

In his documentary movie, *An Inconvenient Truth,* Al Gore pointed out the global warming condition of the world.

Friends, global warming is about the choice of "purity!" If the government and the industrialists will not make the choice of purity, then the people themselves must make it, based on choices of what to buy, consume, eat and support. That is "investing in our future." It is simple choices of what we support that will bring the changes.

The public can become the educators then of the industrial world. If we demand creating only things that bring clean air, water, earth and food, then what is produced will change.

Grassroots decisions create a different grass. This grassroots decision is a public outcry. It is a cry for change. It is the "winds of change" that are upon us. Should we proceed with awareness, it can be as a sweet tropical ocean breeze rather than some of the recent storms and hurricanes. Friends, weather is consciousness. Let us not pretend otherwise. Let us not pretend to be victims of weather. We do not even have to try to awaken. Just be aware and then there is nothing there pretending to sleep.

Purity, my friends, has no opposite. True purity is outside the realm of opposites. It lies not at some whim of shifting around in some duality episode that is sheer belief.

Friends, Purity is calling. It is always calling. It is responding to this call that the "winds of change" are upon us.

Purity is the very presence of the Infinite. We can turn to it.

Move with it. And our old civilization will slip into oblivion as this new culture emerges.

Friends, a culture of purity does stand as revelation!

Saturday, December 23, 2006, 3 a.m. in Maui, Hawaii

A New Communing

Communications are a communing. There is a back and forth balanced sending of information.

Those who dominate do not commune with balance.
They don't commune at all.
They tell; they order; they dictate.

No understanding is achieved. Tyranny births. A little at a time. And born is master/ slave, oppressor/oppressed, victimizer/victim. Slain is balance. Slain is the Universal Law of Balance.

And fear does rear its head. With fear as the player on dominator's field, there is no hope; there is no reciprocity. Self-dominion dies.

And individual expression lies weeping. Weeping for its loss, its imprisonment, its wings of freedom.

Where shall we find these wings of freedom? Consciousness must take flight. Consciousness is all there is. Consciousness must rise above the belief in an unequal, imbalanced world.

Each person must make the journey of consciousness. Each person must bypass flights of fancy and falsity and make flights beyond the suppressive voice of duality. Each person must see and know and live beyond this limited state that would create such opposition and oppression.

This demands a journey of the soul.
This demands a new communication.
This demands a new communing.
This demands a flight into Oneness.
This demands unity consciousness.

And comes…unification.
Endless expressions of balance.
Endless new forms of communication.
Forms the mind has never known.
Forms that stun the mind.

Consider…all forms are light and sound. Do you yet commune with all the forms? Do you hear the rocks, the flowers and the seeming soundless Ones?

Science, technology, intuition, clairvoyance and on can turn attention to communing with the Unheard.

Friends, come, commune.
And wars shall fall away.
Rivers of tears shall be no more.

Together, we shall harness a collective consciousness of sacred communion.

Nature shall sing forth
her Unheard songs…
She shall be heard.

And joy shall fill the air.

July 27, 2006
Written at 11:30 a.m. while driving to Ashland, Oregon

Immortality Calls

Humanity sleeps. Lost in thought. Lost in mortality thinking, planning and preparing. The tombstone may as well be purchased along with life insurance that buys the certainty of death. A death whose expenses are covered. A tidy little package that was a special decades ago. Death becomes a human purpose in life, plodding in a decay ridden body toward that dreadful day. That day that reveals how little was learned in life and about life. That day that asks for what is due. That day that understands cause and effect. That day demands its due. It knows that what we have cast upon the waters of life returns to us. A law that does not change.

O friends…immortality calls.
It calls in the sweetest ways.
Immortality's voice is heard in nature.
The water speaks to us, should we care to hear.
And the herbs of the field.
And sounds…
Sounds of rivers roaring
    and oceans lapping on the sand.

Trees speak, heavy laden with fruit almost reaching
    to the ground asking us to eat.

And the sky…it speaks in tones of blue…
    a recognition of an opening into endless space.
And endless possibilities. Limitation, a word that passes
    from the language, a dinosaur burdening even the book
    of words.

O friends…ask yourselves…
What does an immortal world look like?
What is it that fills its days and fills its nights?

Is any water good?
Do you call for purity?
Do you hasten now to cast your voice for water that is pure? Are
you willing to halt purchases from industries of pollution? Are you
willing to take that stand for a water screaming everywhere to be
heard?

And air thick with darkened space. The tale of our consumption.
How will we live when we've cast a vote for azure skies?
How will we live?

And the earth rumbles and shakes around the globe
reminding us of city dumps and industrial dumps everywhere.
Reminding us of toxic wastes traveling in box cars and semis
to distant places. Towns, villages, cities everywhere pretending
they don't exist.

And people everywhere believing nuclear energy is clean, while
growing tanks of nuclear waste are disgracing now our lands.
We think that if it's out of sight that it exists not.

O friends…immortality calls.
It speaks like a child of purity.
It asks a simple question.
Are you willing to change?
Are you willing to choose purity?
Are you willing to create a world
*   of pure air, pure water and soil.*
Are you willing to begin new tomorrows
*   by choosing purity today?*

Another world doth come.
It carries another insurance.
It insures your joy, your smiles and never-ending dreams.
It insures life everlasting.
And life immortal.

Do you hear? Do you hear immortality's call?
Ever it has known your name.
It knows ever your true name
> *written by Infinity.*
Your name is I.
And everywhere I am.
And that which you see about you and
> *into the farthest reaches of space.*
It is I.
It is I, I say.
It is I.

I am the Immortal that you dream upon…
> *thinking it fantasy on another shore.*
I am not at a distant shore.
I am with you even now.

O ponder well my Presence.
Don the nakedness of your feet and
> *walk upon my earth.*
Walk upon the rocks, the sand.
Soon shall you walk upon the waters of life
> *and see me everywhere.*

Fast upon purity.
You need no guide.
Ever does your soul commune
> *when ears are not flapping in the wind.*
Ever does your soul commune
> *when empty listening fills you full.*

Never more indulge in…I don't know how.
Ask to know.
Open wide to know.
Knowing can pour from ways unseen.
Open now to know.

July 4, 2006, written at 3:15 p.m. at South Fork River in
Mount Shasta, California

Dominion Calls Your Name

What does it mean to have been given dominion? Dominion is from within. Power is within. It is only we, through ignorance or somnolence, that could cause us to give dominion to something or someone or some place in the outer world, the external world. It is we, individually, who must exercise and practice dominion. Should we knowingly or unknowingly give it away, we have still given it away. Our gift from the Infinite given away. Such a gift is precious. It is the answer to a joyful life and a fulfilled life.

Dominion Consciousness does rise above the mortal concepts and opinions of good and bad. It sets in motion the Universal Law of Balance, of equality, of love shared. We are in charge only of our own world…to the degree that we say…yes. That yes is a great treasure in our world. And that yes is a great responsibility in our world.

What shall be our days and what our nights
  should we not say yes to dominion?
We shall create ever in our world scenarios of servitude,
  of victim, of slave or neediness and oppression.
Sad we become blaming ever the outer world for bullying us,
  taking from us, raping and plundering our lives.
This blame would fall into dissolution should we
  answer to self-responsibility.
This blame would have no home.
This blame consciousness would fall away, disappear,
  never to return upon the beauty of our path.

O today…today choose dominion…

Watch the Power of the Infinite arise in your voice,
  in your steps and in the gestures of your day.

Watch the Power play upon the moments of your day.
Watch the joy find a resting place in your heart
  and streaming from your eyes.

Never again lose sight of dominion.
Never again think of it as an outdated world.
Never again dismiss its infinite power granted unto you.
Never again forget.

Such gifts waiting upon our noticing.
Such gifts beckoning a life unimagined and unexplored.
Such gifts calling ever our name.

Come…this day…this moment…dominion calls…

Don't let it pass by yet another time
  while busy hiding from your Self…

Come…friends…come…dominion calls your name…

June 19, 2006, written at 4:40 p.m. at South Fork River, Mount Shasta, California

Everything is perfect just as it is...

Everything is perfect just as it is. You don't believe that? That...is exactly why you are living an imperfect life. You believe...that.

You may believe that or you may entertain the truth, a principle of life. The Universe does not care if you believe it or not. You are quite free to entertain any human thought of good or bad that you choose.

To entertain the thought that everything is perfect as it is takes an expanded consciousness. Otherwise one is making the decision based on the limitations of the human in a sense of separation from Source.

Besides...the mind loves having opinions. And what human wants to give up an opinion, a cherished personal, family, traditional, racial or national belief? How could one feel right or supreme or superior or separate without that belief that deeply engages separation from the Source, from the knowing that we are One?

O no. The human mind would not like to entertain such radical ideas as Oneness. It is accustomed to making differences the very reason for life, for war, for endless personal battles. It is just the way of the human mind which exists as the basis of dualistic thinking.

There are two ways to leave the dualistic thinking which is the cause of all suffering. One is through Grace, such as seen in the sages, masters and saints through the ages. The other is through an expanded awareness. That may take dedication. For the human collective mind divided unmercifully against its very self is deep rooted. The habit has been practiced in the long ages through vanquished empires.

When one is ready, a new practice ensues. Going from the mind to the mindless is the way. From the human mind of concepts to the One Mind. For there is but One Mind. The only seeming exception is the human belief in good and bad.

Oh how hard and difficult it is for the human mind to embrace this truth. It will attempt to capture you in great debate and argument with self or others. It will not die easily. It does not like such expressions as "you must die daily."

Just what does "die daily" mean? It means to give up, release your judgments, opinions, concepts, that is, your belief in good and evil. How exactly did we walk out of the garden, the paradise world, the nirvana of the Mind? We embodied duality, the belief in good and evil. And we have been paying the price ever since.

We chase the good (pleasure) and we run from or battle evil (pain). Chasing after or running from. That is the human condition.

Should we catch even a glimpse outside of these human beliefs, then we have been touched by the mindless One. Pure awareness begins to find its way into our lives.

Grace arrives.

We may go back and forth between the human mind and the One Mind on a daily basis for many years. Here is where the power of Desire does dance into our lives. Should we Desire the One Mind, then we shall find our personal way to embrace It. And It will embrace us.

That embrace of the Infinite is the Supreme we have been looking for. There is a Supreme and it wants to live as our very lives. It is the endless supply of joy, love, friends. It is the endless supply of everything. It is the infinite supply of your fulfillment.

Perfection.
Perfection Is.
That is it. Embrace it or not.
Casting it away is a call for endless suffering.
One can only prove the perfection in the living of the principle.
To desire to live the principle, there must be a feeling,
a consciousness, that this is so.

The world is now being peopled with a new race of awakening ones. These people are not living in this human world of belief of good and evil. They live in "another world." They increasingly live in a paradise world, side by side with those still in opposition, battle and war. Those in opposition live in a divided world. And there is pain. And rage. And hate. Fear. And these are ever indulged in, in the mind, emotions and even the actions of the body.

So come. Come unto perfection. Remove yourself from these beliefs in good and evil that still do bind you. That imprison you. It is only difficult in the beginning. Your mind is so entrenched in the entertainment of the epic human battle in endless forms though the ages.

The mind does look around and finds no place to engage. It is bored. Where is the action? Where is something happening? Where is the spouting of opinions?

A new world does borne.
It is an individual journey back to the home of the One Mind.
Love.
It is the enchantment and delight we all do look for in this seeming outer world. And always, it was in the One Mind.

And change it comes. It comes galloping on the horse of Life. For Life…it comes from within. It is our very Self externalized.

Enjoy everywhere…the one Self.

Truly it is in the deep desire for this perfection that we understand the principle and how to practice it. Through desire, we will have the dedication to practice, to become aware of another world. That world is a world of consciousness, of awareness and it does birth the garden of your dreams.

That world does beckon. It beckons in every movement of life. Every sound. Even the rocks do beckon. Are we listening? It is everywhere. And it beckons.

Come…

Wednesday, February 22, 2006
Driving from Taos to Santa Fe in the a.m.

*The title, *Everything is perfect just as it is,* began to come to me as I began driving. Joy began to fill me. As my mind immediately tried to deny that all was perfect, I found myself agreeing with it all on a deep feeling level. And the words in the passage began to flow.

Silence HER No More

*In the following passage, woman is the metaphor for the divine feminine, the yin, in woman and in man.

*As I lay awake, silent and empty in the night, these words did begin to come:

Silence Her no more. Silence HER no more. Silence Her no more.

....

We have all seen this following scenario or, if a woman, perhaps have done this or at least wanted to. There is a public meeting or a gathering or perhaps just the simple meeting of a husband or wife or man and woman.

And woman begins to cry. Emotions begin to soar and expand. Even anger begins to appear. In a moment woman is either sobbing, wailing or screaming torrents of livid words.

People are appalled. People are embarrassed. Man, in a mental fashion, sometimes bereft of emotions and feelings, calls for woman to be arrested or even taken away or sometimes even "put away."

Woman in this emotional state is silenced. She is not listened to, not considered. Only the flare is observed. Woman has burst like a volcano and nobody wants to know, nobody wants to see and certainly nobody wants to hear.

I recently heard first-hand about such an outburst. It happened in Los Alamos, New Mexico. It was a public meeting regarding the burying of tanks of nuclear waste, currently stored under tents, unfenced and unguarded in any way.

This woman, whom everyone deemed a spectacle, went to

the front of the audience and fell dramatically to her hands and knees in a praying position and publicly screamed that everyone needed to do likewise and pray that these tanks do not get buried where they can leak and pollute the water supply in a large area.

The crowd that was gathered agreed with the woman and loudly applauded her. She was the collective voice for the sentiments and feelings of most. Those officiating silenced her and told her she would be arrested and taken away if there was another outburst from her.

That act silenced also the crowd who were now afraid to speak out. For they knew the outcome. The mind in separation from Spirit had spoken.

Friends, I tell you, Woman has been silenced too long and too many times. Woman has deep feelings. These feelings are connected to Spirit, to the Creator of us all.

And, I say, Woman has something to say.

Woman, the feeling feminine, is silenced when the man world, the mind, does not want to hear. Woman is silenced when man wants to rape, control and dominate nature, by not only cutting down the forests and jungles of the world, but by putting filth and contaminates into the air and chemicals into the water, rivers and lakes. We have polluted not only our air and water, but our earth and food supply. We even allow our government and the FDA and others to make this legal.

And we have allowed and still allow the creating of agonizing pain for the animals. Farm animals. Sport animals. Domestic animals. Zoo animals. Animals for an endless stream of agonizing experiments and testing. Even the raising of animals for organs. All manners of cruelty. Cages of every kind.

And Woman cries. And Woman screams. And nobody wants to hear.

These very outbursts are warnings. These women are messengers from the divine for the collective ear that we are going, as a humanity, ever further into the hell realms of separation from Spirit, from love. Woman is a loud reminder that we have made a mistake and that we are moving in the wrong direction.

Woman is a messenger from a faraway realm of love, of kindness, of caring.

And nobody wants to hear.

Woman is silenced.

I tell you, friends, silencing of the women is a mistake. Woman is the barometer of the society. She is a revelator.

Woman is the caring Voice of Nature.

And nobody wants to hear.

The collective is too busy stampeding down the road of progress, of getting or having ever more and more and more.

I tell you friends, this collective is empty. It is forlorn and empty and it thinks that it will be happy with more. It then accelerates the rate of consuming and getting and taking.

The world is sick.
The human world is in separation from Life itself.

And Woman tries to warn.

And now comes a shift.
No longer can she be silenced.
This knowing, that has no name, does rise.

This fury shall rise in the oceans and in the skies and in the very bowels of the Earth.

This is SHE. This is The Mother.

We did not listen, nor did we hear, when The Mother spoke through sobbing, saddened, wailing woman.

Now The Mother roars. She roars through nature. No longer does she feign ignorance. Mankind has raped and pillaged so long and broken the laws of nature's balance for so long that now does The Mother rise…bringing balance in her wake.

Friends, are you listening?

Do you compost?
Do you recycle?
Do you eat clean food and drink clean water?
Do you make conscious choices?
Do you consider the animals?
Do you give them a voice?
Do you hear?
Do you listen to the air, to the wind and to the water?
Do you listen to the voice of fire?
Do you give them voice?

O friends, I say, the Voice of Nature speaks and we hear not. She has spoken for eons through Woman and Woman has been silenced.

And now it is. We shall listen to The Mother or we shall pay the price. We are already paying the price. For we are breaking inviolate laws.

But we don't want to hear.
We don't want to know.

I tell you friends. There is a better way. We need not travel down yet another road to self-destruction.

We can align with Nature. We can move and breathe and act in harmony with all of Nature. We can dance the dance of Oneness.

It does not take decades of science or PhDs to see the direction to go.

It is simple. Friends, I say, it is simple. Even a child can know.

The starting questions regarding all creations are these. Is there caring for the Earth? Do our actions maintain the balance of all of nature? That is to say, does the action pollute the air, the water, the earth or the food? Does it pollute or harm the precious animals, the forests, the plants, the people? Do our actions maintain the purity? Do our actions maintain the harmony?

Friends, we must start to ask the right questions. We must ask the right questions in all of our actions.

We must want to know.

One step at a time, by each person, we can turn this nightmare around.

We can choose to live in harmony.
We can have a pure Earth.
We can allow Woman to have a Voice, to guide and point the way.

It is time to Silence Her no more!
She has been crying and shouting through the ages.
She has been screaming about the imbalance.

Upon the scene now arrives The Mother.
Another time does come.
The Voice of Nature speaks.

Friends, SHE speaks whether we welcome her or not.

She brings a fury.
She, unlike woman, cannot be silenced.

She is Life.
She announces herself.
She acts like a tempest and will not stop until heard.
She is the protectress, the guardian of all of Life.

Friends, we are that Life.
It is time, now finally, after eons of not listening to her speak
through woman, to listen.

Nature speaks that the law of balance has been broken.
Are we listening?

The Mother has come.

Silence her no more.

Sunday, December 18, 2005
Written at 12:50 a.m. in Taos, New Mexico

The Secular as Sacred

Thomas Paine said, "Give me liberty or give me death." I am not sure that it has to be one or the other. But there are some serious considerations here.

Ed Murrow, the truth journalist of the 50s, lost his television anchorman job because of telling the truth. The TV station owner wanted to entertain the people, because that did not stir up anything with politicians. In other words, keep the public placated via "not knowing" even while "corruption" acts out its imbalances and hurts many innocent people in its lying and thieving wake. Is this the world that we want to live in?

Ed Murrow and all of the others who helped him bring the news that exposed lies and injustice lost their jobs. Sometimes there is a price to pay for telling the truth. But isn't there even a bigger collective price to be paid by the public for staying in ignorance?

And who is responsible for demanding the truth? The people. The public. The collective. We are the ones. Are we too much in fear and trembling to call to know the truth? Are we too afraid that our social time will get swallowed up while calling to know the truth? Why has not the public unified in a way that protects individual rights and freedoms to know the truth? Wasn't that the role of the government, which is actually performing just the opposite act? Something is direly wrong here. A new direction must be found.

Thomas Merton, the modern Trappist monk, revealed to all of us, in his 27 years of retreat from the world, that there is no retreat from the world. He came to the realization that there was no division between the sacred and the secular. And he spent his life revealing many of the same things that

Ed Murrow did. That truth, values, justice, must be a part of all life, no matter what is the sector of society. Truth is sacred and it must be lived in all parts of what we imagine to be a secular world. Corruption has no place, for it exploits the lives of others and takes away from their rights as individuals. Thus it takes away the liberty of the individual.

So "give me liberty or give me death."
Is that the only choice?

LIBERTY is Life itself.
Liberty is a Life fully spontaneous, fully free.
Liberty is sacred. It is our truth lived.
And it is a right in all aspects of Life.
Thus let us realize that the secular and sacred are one.

Written on November 30, 2005

Voice for the Animals:
Another world does beckon...

I have heard the words "I don't want to know" many times, for many years, from many people, from many places. I have heard these words when I begin to tell any stories of the needless and horrific suffering of animals in all sectors of societies around the globe. I ask people if they know. Many do say, "No, I don't want to know."

Now...I say to anyone who says "I don't want to know," why do you not want to know? Why exactly do you not want to know?

Do you not want to know because you will have to admit the truth and no longer be in denial?

Do you not want to know because you will feel guilty, individually and/or collectively?

Do you not want to know because you will have to consider what actions to take?

Do you not want to know because it might mean change?

Do you not want to know because you will have to be conscious of what you support?

Do you not want to know because it means taking responsibility for what you support?

Do you not want to know because the implication of responsibility is vast?

Do you not want to know because of the stocks and funds you have invested in that direction?

Do you not want to know because of the social implications with friends and relatives?

Do you not want to know because there are too many more important issues on personal, national or global levels?

I say, my friends, we are the animals.

Bestowing pain on a living being is the antithesis of love.

I say, my friends, we must find new ways.
We must find new ways to love the animals.
All animals.

We must find new ways to relate to these animals.
We must awaken to the sacredness of the animals.
We must awaken to the soul of the animals.

Cruelty to the animals is our cruelty.
Cruelty to the animals is in our country and around the globe.
Cruelty to the animals is quite literally in our backyard.
It is in our kitchen.
It is in our lives.
And we have accepted it as the integral fabric of our society.
And it is sad.
And few there are who want to talk about it.
Keep it in the "industries" and don't let the information leak.
Whitewash it all, so we can all pretend.
So we can pretend and live the lie with no responsibility.
So we can stay children in some fabricated dream world.

Another world does beckon…

In each heart and each soul is a vision of that world.
No one can tell us what It is.
We, ourselves, must open to It.
We, ourselves, must ask to see.
It is initially a solitary journey.

The changes…they do come.

Consider this…

What if?

What if adults watched movies of the current terror wreaked on wild and domestic animals around the world?

What if adults eating, wearing or using animals took annual tours through the industries' farms, holding pens and slaughter houses?

What if adults eating, wearing or using animals watched the documentaries of animal treatment and conditions?

What if mainstream media began to cover these issues instead of jumping in bed with the industries and hiding it all from public view?

What if there was no more hiding or denying what is going on with the animals around the globe?

What if adults "were put in cages or pens" to see what it feels like, that zoos, aquariums and such could cease?

And…
What if the children knew?

And…
If the children knew, what would they do?
What would they say?
How would they feel about their parents?
How would they feel about their society?

A new world…it does come…

A world where finally the animals are safe…
A world where finally the animals are happy…
A world where animals are respected…

A world where animals are honored…listened to…
A world where animals are acknowledged as part of the one Soul…

A new world…it does come…

Following is a little bit of my story of awakening to the plight of the animals. Bit by bit it unraveled in my life.

When my children were very young, I already knew what was happening to the animals. I tried to find sensitive ways to share the truth with them about how much pain and suffering was created for animals. That was especially hard. Since the industrializing of farms there has been the massive horrors and terrors created for the farm animals in the raising and slaughtering of them. My children looked at me with pained expressions and said, "I don't want to know. It hurts to know." I could always understand, after that, that children are innocent and totally naïve to the brutal and inhumane ways of this current society. And they are ultra-sensitive to feeling. Full empaths. Children have not yet habituated in the mind, nor have they numbed themselves literally senseless. They are vulnerable and don't expect such barbaric and insidious facts from the adult world around them. It literally is too much for a tender psyche. I understand.

Then years later, in meditation, I began to be lifted in consciousness to the Soul Realms of the animals. They revealed themselves as already Christed. And they informed me wordlessly that they were awaiting humanity to come into the direct knowing of Oneness. They know we are One. Now it is time for humanity to know.

As these inner journeys of being lifted into the illumined animal realms continued, I began to revisit my own childhood sensitivity to the animals. I spoke to them. I listened to them.

They were my friends. I sat for hours upon hours with crabs, squirrels, stray dogs, injured birds. I rode the giant sea turtles. I raised my own rooster that I loved dearly. I found endless birds with broken wings or ones who left the nest too soon. They needed someone to feed them and protect them until they could fly. That I did.

My family was from Iowa, heartland of America. I had many farming relatives. They had farm animals that were treated with respect. My grandmother had a small chicken farm. Those chicks were raised in freedom and dignity. They had the run of the farm.

From childhood, I was raised as a carnivore. Though I could not bear to see a chicken having its neck wrung, I still had no idea of the meat and poultry and fish "industry" that was growing around the country and globe. I had no idea of the endless brutal and inhumane practices that were growing. I had no idea yet of the tortured lives of these precious animals living by the multimillions.

I first began to awaken to the sadistic industrial practices developing in the sixties. I became aware of the cruelty to the farm animals in 1960, when I took my first visit to an Iowa chicken farm. I was aghast at the sights, smells, conditions. I was horrified at the suffering of these precious beings with barely any room to move. I could barely stand to know. I felt the pain of the animals. Some of us have not become numbed out and still have our ability to empath, to feel.

It was 1960. What did I do? Nothing. Absolutely nothing. I blocked it. I put it out of my mind. Remember the adage... out of sight...out of mind? Well it works. At least for a while. I went away to college, received my degree, found an English teaching position and had babies. Sounds most familiar. That all American state of somnolence. Just way too busy to ever take another inner or outer look at the plight of these sweet souls.

By 1971, I continued to awaken, with the help of a head-on car collision that lifted me into the Now, where past, present and future are already One and all is Soul Joy of Being. I quit my college English instructor position, got a divorce and went traveling, going overland across the Middle East and ending in Kashmir and India. I wanted to find my own way of realizing my true identity, my Self. I began praying and meditating to rise above the realm of fear and enter again the Here and Now.

Then one day in New Delhi, in the midst of smells, noise, cars, busses, trucks, animals, people and rickshaws, a solitary cow did change my life. This cow walked across a busy street, ignoring all the endless activity, straight toward me. Communion. That cow succeeded in soul to soul contact through the eyes. I was now a vegetarian. From that moment. Something was transmitted and I changed. No words can convey what happened in that exchange. The sublime. The Unspoken. I certainly now understood the words…holy cow.

So back to the statement, "I don't want to know." By the nineties I was hearing many adults saying "I don't want to know" when I would try to bring up the animal suffering. Some would even tell me that I was making them feel guilty personally and as a human for inflicting this pain. It was as though if I did not bring it up, it did not exist. A grand pretending.

I then went through a period where I quit talking about it. I continued to read and learn what was happening to the animals. Farm animals, the fish, animals used for testing and experiments. The wild animals. The circus animals. The animals everywhere in cages. Zoos, bird cages, indoor and outdoor aquariums. Animal farms for organs, body parts, urine, etc. for a diseased humanity. Animals, both wild and

118

caged for the clothing industry. The list is much, much longer.

I began to wonder.

Why is it so few want to know?
Why is it they want to ignore the obvious?
Why is it they want everyone to shut up and pretend it is not happening?
Why is it they don't care?

I began to wonder.

I wondered if humans were so habituated into this all that they did not want to change.

I wondered if humanity so loved the known animal tastes that it would refuse to give them up.

I even wondered if the human mind was so clever in its ability to deny, that if it could keep everyone quiet about the obvious, it could pretend this cruelty did not exist.

I wondered if this Pollyanna attitude could just talk about fashion, the newest latte, the latest model car, the second home, etc. and just sweep all that is not glamorous into a dark collective corner of the consciousness, where everyone could just choose to believe that it simply was not happening. Conscience has little voice under such a thick veneer.

I ignored it all for years, so I do understand. I "believed" I would not be safe and secure in life if I did not do certain things. I needed to get my degree. I needed to get married. I needed to get a job. I needed to raise my children. There was always a need bigger than the subject of obscene brutality and bestial actions being wreaked upon these vulnerable souls.

I would ask myself…where is the conscience of humanity?
I would ask myself…where are the feelings of humanity?

I would ask myself…where is the soul of humanity and the heart?

And then it was I who saw that I needed to give the animals a voice.
These beings had no voice of their own.
Gradually I determined that I would speak.

Even in the 90s came many passages from Spirit and from the Soul of the animals. I created a recording called *Return to Oneness* to begin to both give a voice to the animals and to allow listeners to find their ability to feel and empath.

All that has been spoken here cannot be pushed onto a free will humanity so lost in a sense of separation from the realization of Oneness. We can only be an example, be a voice for those with no voice, educate and ask within what our role is in relation to the precious animal kingdom. And we can be aware of this "sad appearance" world as its "true identity as already a spiritual universe."

Another world does beckon…

November 27, 2005, Taos, New Mexico

Keepers of the Balance

O the irony of it all as a hurricane named Rita comes crashing in on the gulf coast, carrying the energy of the thought forms of the oil greed consciousness that formed it…and heading straight, for the second time in a month, toward the oil consciousness/rigs and equipment that created the heat and conditions that created the hurricanes.

How is it that these hurricanes can be called destructive? They are merely the mechanisms of nature to rebalance herself. They are nature's form of justice. They are merely nature perfectly rebalancing herself. They are merely her reaction to man's actions of imbalance and selfishness. They are fully impersonal.

And we see it not.

Sadness fills the air as Nature gives the lesson of action/reaction in order to enact and live on this plane of existence the grand and primordial principle of balance.

Shall this be the great aha for humanity as this inviolate Law of Balance reveals to us all that it has been violated?

We have before us, not the task of rebuilding just cities and people's precious lives.

We have before us the daunting task of shifting the consciousness of humanity. Of revealing that this inexorable law of balance is the law of love. And that this love is equal giving and regiving.

That law of balance has built into its very self…justice and equality for all.

O those of little minds or selfish minds do see it not, so full of self are they.

It matters not. Nature stands supreme. She is the very principle of balance in action. And now does she do a simple action. She balances that which has brought imbalance. And she shall repeat herself endlessly until we do choose to harmonize with her.

It is not complicated. It is simple.
And humanity sees it not.
And humanity thinks it is the wrath of nature or of the gods, or even worse, of God.

It is us and we see it not. God is the Law of Balance, of love, and we see it not.

No wonder that, in addition, the hurricane winds would go straight toward the creations of the oil greed consciousness that created it. A simple enough message should we care to read the signs.

No wonder also that New Orleans was affected. A community of many caught right at ground zero of the greed consciousness in the pits of the poverty created by this very imbalance.

Amazing how Nature in her pristine balance can expose so many injustices and imbalances so quickly, with no words, no long debates, not even an argument or a war or a battle.

It is amazing how she is demanding that America take some attention off its war in Iraq and focus on her own imbalance, her own wrongdoings.

Friends, this is not doomsday or Armageddon. This is pure science. This is the simple reaction of Nature to our actions. There is no mystery here.

And we can turn it around before it is too late if we choose to.

Certainly there is no doubt that now is the time.

Complacency has worn its face for too long.
And denial has kept us asleep.

We have before us not so much the left and the right wings,
the republicans and the democrats, etc.
We have before us consciousness…"awake and asleep."

Those who have awakened or are now awakening are people
who put vision in action. They live the law of balance and
share with others how to do so.

The Law of Balance.
It is time.

The principle of love.
It is time.

The global understanding of actions and equal reactions.
It is time.

Those simple things enacted are
the dance of love on this planet.

That dance of love includes all of nature.
It includes all the people, the animals, the plants, the minerals.
It includes the water, the air, the earth.

It is simple.
We are one.

We are the dance of love
And we see it not.

We are that very dance of love.

May the reactions of Nature to keep the Balance
sober us and give us the needed understanding
of this process of Nature that shall not be stopped
by human fears and selfishness and greed.

May the reactions of Nature to keep the Balance
reveal to us that we must be the *"keepers of the balance."*
We are not the controllers of Nature.
We are not in charge.

Let us this day harmonize and be at One
with this precious Balance.
It is a living Presence.
We can feel it.
We can join into this dance of love.

Now is the time.
Let us be at One.
We are that.

Saturday, September 24, 2005, written at 4:30 a.m.

The Unseen Garden

I wondered for years why I deeply disliked history in high school. Years later I thought perhaps it was because I was right brained and more of an essence and aerial view person, rather than obsessed with memory and parroting of wars, their dates, places and names of violent war lords. And I could further never understand the American tourist urge to visit all the national war sites commemorating our battles with Indians and with each other, as in the Civil War. At each stage of awakening I was witnessing a nation fascinated with war and war history. One hears the expression "get a life" said to people who have seemingly no life of their own. It seems our nation and others could also be prompted on this cosmic stage to "get a life."

Then even later I realized that the history books were filled with many lies, filled with accounts told by the so-called victor of the war. And I began to ask, "Are these victories? Were they ever victories?"

Why have none of our national leaders, who see the United States as a world leader, been leading our country and our world down the path of peace? And who dare say that war and peace are opposites? Whosoever does not understand that peace is a state of consciousness, not a state of "momentary no war," has not gone deep enough, has not called up the memory of "the unseen garden." No, it is not some faraway place in the distant past. No, it is not some idyllic and fantasized future. It lies in neither of those never to be reached destinations. In fact, it simply is not a destination. It is a state of consciousness. It is. And to dwell in this land we must go deep within.

It is there we will discover that human war and human peace

are temporary creations of the ever human mind, a duality that we no longer need. A duality that never did we need.

Forging ahead as heinous and sinister war mongers claiming we are doing it in the name of peace is the pastime of a fool. It is the pastime of insanity.

Living humanity's sojourn through duality has been a poor choice. All of this in the name of greed and fear. Ever wanting more. The irreverent chant is "booty." And that booty has included raping and killing and selling of women and children. And in case some of the history is true, even the Indians stole women from other tribes in the night. I never did read a story of a raid by women to steal men in the night. It appears to be a gender issue, but one has to be careful of not sounding like a feminist. It is not trendy. Never has been.

The word civilization is a misnomer. Diabolic nations often fit the description, if truth be spoken. It seems that when some write a public record, it is called history. When others speak of it, it is called feminist. Seems there is a bias. And one's popularity diminishes if you dare even whisper certain truths.

Sure, there are endless hamlets, villages and towns across our nation and the world filled with simple and loving people who want peace. But often in that childlike innocence, these peaceful souls do give the responsibility to war lords and dictators though they often wear benign names such as governor, president or king.

The people (just common people) must awaken and find new ways to take responsibility. Many are still floundering and their lives are drowning in their own ignorance.

And many have awakened and do awaken. It is through these light filled lives that we shall see local, national and even global changes. What have these people awakened to?

Certainly not to the demise of this suffering world of endless torment.

They have awakened to the unseen. This unseen vision flashes as an indomitable fire in their hearts. This unseen vision becomes the foundation of a new world when all do leave mental adages like "you are your brother's keeper." These words do cease to be words and birth as illumined actions of love.

The unseen world is seen.

The unseen garden does appear.

Paradox is shown...

June 7, 2004, written while driving on highway 40 from Flagstaff to Albuquerque

Authentic Animation

Is there any wonder why men and women have so much anger for one another? Is there any wonder why we have wars? Is there any wonder about the personal and global effects of man/woman imbalance on the planet? It is and has been devastating. We can be the consciousness that is the solution to the problem.

Women and men…of the world…gather together in the name of the One. It matters not your race, creed, religion. Know only that we are a part of the wordless, nameless One. In that…we become a coalescing force…for unity consciousness, for oneness consciousness…without which we continue to have wars, battles, struggles, suffering and strife.

This is a simple principle. It is an inviolate principle. Ponder the word inviolate. We must walk from the battle and enter into the Silence. There…in the Silence…are the first stirrings of authentic animation from Cause.

Do not be pulled into the battle of effects.
It is futile.
It has been the battle of the ages.
It has played out on the bloody stage of humanity's tears.

We can dance on another stage.
That stage is the playground borne of a deep Silence…
Peace that Is…Balance that Is…
We each have a part…
Let us begin this day…
Let us create illumined moments…

September 18, 2003
Written at the river in Mount Shasta, California

Heroes and Heroines

We make heroes and heroines out of those with a great cause, running around trying to save the world. Some are trying to save it with technology with such things as cloning and stem cell research. Others are trying to save it with natural ways. At opposite ends of the spectrum…both believe they are right. And the battle goes on.

While the Law of Nature rules and reigns supreme, what is lost here is the realization that there is nothing to save. The world is. And she balances herself.

The true heroes and heroines are those who achieve the awareness of Being, who realize the Balance that already is. They are the ones who attune to that Balance in all of Nature.

They are the ones who begin to live in that harmony.

All the running around like madmen and women will cease in this realization. The ever human mind cannot save the world. The heroic pioneers of the New Way take flight beyond the mind. Peace is Known. Peace is shared. The Law of Balance understood.

Heroic only are the ones who realize the Supreme.
All others play in the realm of thoughts of the finite game.
Time and space allows for such games.
Human games.

The Supreme just watches…for time and space…they never were.

August 8, 2001
Written at 3:45 p.m. while driving to San Francisco

The Waiting Place

She awakens. There is no light in the sky. Yet morning comes. Her feet silently touch the floor. Soft loose clothing wrap her as she drives to the waiting place. A winding forest road seems not to end.

She wonders at her morning journey beneath the starlit sky. No other one is there. She breathes in the light from a place beyond the mind and all the world. She feels it sweep away her fears, concerns and problems hanging in her mind. They have little hold and cannot grasp her mind. She sighs. The thoughts have vanished again.

She stops at the waiting place. This is where the Sun does greet the day, and night does fade away as if it never were. She smiles. She loves this place, high above the village floor.

She breathes again. Joy does fill the very morning air. She wonders if this joy that seems to have no cause is merely fantasy. It has no cause. No reason has it any. It has no goal. There is no destination. Purpose...it has none.

O this joy...as a mountain flower...which knows no eyes... grows only in the peace...deep in a silence borne of stillness...

The waiting place...

July 29, 2001

At dawn, I am driving home from an art exhibit in Truckee, California. A story comes to me during an exceptional and spectacular sunrise, that seems to be in very slow motion.

About Prophecies

Dear friends, below is a passage that came to me from Spirit in the late eighties about prophecies. It seems that in light of what is occurring on the planet that the message is potent today. It is a passage from my book, *Galactic Shamanism,* about the Earth Changes now happening…

Prophecies are Messengers of Change

The years come and the years go. Many there are among you who rise above the day-to-day prattle of human life and who see far into the human future, the perennial handwriting on the wall. Because there are so very many imbalanced actions of miscreation, born out of separation from ME…the Infinite ONE, these flights into the human future are often very grim, for they are based on actions presently lived. These flights are called prophesies…and they are nigh filled with warnings, messages of needed change…or comes…impending disaster, destruction and doom.

But these prophetic messages are nothing but timely prewarnings. Prophesies are "messengers" of change. They are not harbingers of disaster, of Armageddons predicted and destined. They are fate only for those who look away, ignore and refuse to change.

For those who refuse to change, change comes anyway and blows across lives…sweetly, moving some as a willow tree and breaking unyielding ones, fraught with crystallizing seasons' past.

For those who change, when the warning doth "wave its flag," the flight of fiendish vision never comes. The prophecy for them does leave no tracks…ere their lives no longer foretell a future of good fortune gone astray.

Rather do the lives of untold persons become a Light unto the world. A Light that also is a flight into the future. This future is the ever searched for Garden that can never be reached by map. This future is the present lived in love.

This is the only prophecy of Truth. It looks beyond the fields of miscreation and sees another world. A world of Heaven-sent visions...thus heaven-sent prophecy. The choice is clearly to be made by each individual with free will choice as it is.

The most that each individual can do is to live the inner vision that they see. Each vision lived will complete a piece of the grander picture and cause others to see their part of the ONE vision. And one by one, then two by two, in ever increasing numbers will the vision of the ONE be fulfilled. No workshop, book or teacher can give one this. It is a solitary flight to the vision of the ALL.

Nature and the Arts:
Art as Consciousness

Any one of us may journey back in time to explore ancient cultures and "see" revealed on cave walls, pottery, temples and jewelry the connection between the arts, consciousness and nature. That they are interconnected and interrelated from these times is a certainty. Even...they are one expression. We are the very trees, the very flowers, the very mountains that be. We are the very nature that we paint, sculpt, draw, dance, sing.

I was fortunate as a child to have nature as my friend, comforter and teacher. I climbed trees, swung from vines across deep ravines, rode sea turtles, made friends with crabs and squirrels who revealed their lives. I ran through the water element in deep ditches during heavy rain storms in Iowa, carried by the swift movement. I lived much precious time in trees eating fruits and nuts and feeling embraced by the arms that are limbs. In nature, I was home. At that time, I had no words like Soul, Spirit, Presence and on. Yet it is certain that what I was feeling was the Soul of all of Nature.

While I always loved drawing and dance and other art expressions from childhood, by the time I was in my twenties, I could no longer see a future as an English teacher or a coordinator in public educational television. I went back to the university for another degree...fine arts.

Artistic expression is a deep calling from the Soul. When feeling deep Oneness with Nature, with the Earth and all her inhabitants, one is often filled with song, dance, poetry, images. It is here that we can move to the ecstatic feeling of expression in the arts. Expression can supersede all suppressions, oppressions, compressions and depressions. The pressure then is only the bursting forth of the joys of feeling nature. What exaltation is felt as we begin to express from our own Self, our heart and soul. Beauty revealed.

In my own journey of drawing, painting, printmaking, sculpting from my deepest Self, I found immense changes happening in my outer life. The inner, formless life that is Spirit and outer form of Life were no longer seen as having a great chasm, abyss, separation.

As the years passed, I needed to keep paper and pen beside me as I painted. For in painting, I am in Presence, feeling the heart, and the flow of poetry and revelations begins to come. These in turn become passages and poetic odysseys of Divine Consciousness and Awareness. These become books. I then learned from my heart how to teach a form of what I call Galactic Shamanism where I initiate and navigate Journeys through the Kingdoms (of the Earth) and Journeys through the Elements. These, in turn, bring heightened awareness of our Oneness in this illumined web of creation. We are One.

All of this seems to have arisen from painting from my Soul. Expressing from the Soul is a portal, a window, door, opening to the Self. The True Self. In that, we find that our self is the One Self. In that, we find that the personal story is the Impersonal Life.

As the new Earth, the new culture, emerges we need to express from the heart. The left brain paradigm wandered away from Balance, from the Dance of the One. True art is soul art and opens the right brain illumination and genius. We are inspired. And Beauty…she does come…

The lost art has been the loss of the "art of feeling." The heart feeling nature, especially in the wild, is a return to "the feelings."

This is a prerequisite for our Earth, that is one living organism, to be in balance. We must open to "feeling."

In that. the illumination is there. The spark to create is there. The "direct knowing" is there. The imagination soars taking flight to realms of joy. Inspiration is there.

And while the thinking mind has no access, it can carry out the expression, giving form. And Balance…Love…it is known.

Vision Gathering for the New Culture

Vision is not something to argue or debate.
Vision is something that lives inside to be lived.
It is a guiding light.
It is the Mystical to be made manifest.
It has a vibration, a frequency.
It can be felt.
Align only with that felt frequency.

In 1971, I began to be uplifted into the new Earth realms of potential. What to do with these experiences? I painted and I sculpted and wrote.

In Vision, it seems like the future being seen.
In other languaging, it is the unrealized present (Potential) that sits waiting when one is not caught in worry and fear about jobs, bankruptcy, scarcity and on.

This is a time to put one foot in front of the other, fulfilling one's highest Vision.

Vision for the new Earth culture:

It is said that people with no vision do perish.
I would like to speak about Vision.
We are all visionaries.
But not all have opened the inner vision.
Why do we even need to do that, one might ask.
Because the world is within, I say.
The world is within.

I began my first deep flight into "the new Earth consciousness" strongly by 1971. These journeys into the realms of the real have continued.

I have opened, witnessed, felt and experienced much of the Potential waiting for humanity.

In this realm (a state of Consciousness), there is no fear.
In this realm, there is no society built around economy or fear of not having enough. Or fear of anything.

It is a world based on decisions made for the good of the Whole. (Not just for people, but the Earth, her kingdoms and her elements.)

It is a world based on purity. Purity of water, air, soil and food.

It is a world based on this inviolate universal principle: The Law of Balance, which is the law of nature, which is the law of love.

This then would be a world of giving and regiving. This is the principle that has been violated. It is why there is poverty of individuals, cities and nations.

Giving and regiving. What does that even mean?
It is the masculine and feminine principle in balance.
It is the yin and the yang in balance.
For 6000 years there has been an imbalance.

Each person who finds the new Earth will find it in Consciousness within. Then the seeming mystical may be made practical.

Vision is something only found in each heart and soul.
It will never be found by a fearful looking outside ourselves and trying to fix a broken local and global economy based on false and imbalanced values.

Those times are complete.

They are unsustainable.
Those things did not work.

The new Earth is a world based on new values.
The feminine values (of man and woman) are coming into play.
A Dance of Oneness.
Beauty, equality, love, caring for the Earth and her kingdoms and her elements. And feeling. We must learn to feel.

The new Earth is inclusive, not exclusive.

Example: For my vision, EarthCare Global TV, I have done much researching. In the book about the Google Guys, they had a new Earth ideal. That one ideal has benefited humanity like few others. Their ideal was to keep the internet free. Every other search engine wanted to charge for entry to the internet. They had great strength in protecting their vision. They went against all the old rules. They saw humanity with equal access to free information. Their values led the way. They did not even know how to start or run a business. They had a vision for the good of the Whole.

We each carry a piece of that vision for the new Earth. It does not resemble the conflagration of the corporate role model of the past.

Money does not rule. The giving and regiving principle of love/balance rules. It is inviolate. That principle creates abundance. Abundance is created in new ways. Abundance is understood in new ways.

May the strength of our individual Visions create a world that is for the good of the Whole, be that the community, animals, water and on.

The new Earth is by people creating from their hearts and souls. Their expression will flow from within. People will no longer have minimum wage jobs that are just filling the slots of the corporate idea of self gain and greed. People did not birth upon this planet to fulfill somebody else's idea.

Example: When my children were very young and I was growing in my art world, I took a position at a college. In the tutoring department, I became master tutor. Not because I did my job well. I broke all the rules and followed my heart. The library was filled with huge and endless volumes of what was happening in the market place. The students were invited to look through them. For instance, they would see the types of jobs needed by GM or others and begin to study to fill the slot.

It is no wonder they needed a tutor for a learning block.

I would sit them down and ask them what was in their heart. What had they always wanted to do, be. They were shocked. They said no one had ever asked them that. I held space for them to find "the new Earth vision" that they carry. And their lives did change.

Let us all consider these visions for the new Earth. They are a path to the unspeakable joy.

Giving Air a Voice

One can study online and watch DVDs to see and hear many of the possible reasons that chemtrails are happening in the skies across the nation. One can find out the metals and chemicals that are being showered upon the Earth, the animals, the plants and the populace. And for the most part that populace is ignorant of what is going on in our skies.

From all of the research that I have done since 1997, I feel that there are two points which are part of a deep concern that must be considered by the citizens, not only of this area, but across the nation and across the world.

They are this:

1. The citizens of America were given certain public trust rights to unspoiled air and water after the American Revolution, known as The Commons. One of those rights is the right to pure air. Robert F. Kennedy Jr., who wrote *Crimes Against Nature,* speaks about this in his book.

    I do not believe that the people of this nation would consciously choose to put toxins of any nature into the air to shower down upon our bodies, our water supply, our food supply and the Earth and all her precious inhabitants. The problem that we have here is that the populace has not been educated and asked if this is ok. Why not, I ask?

2. The second point is this: There is a universal Law of Balance in all of nature. It is understood by scientists. It is inviolate and inexorable. And should we break that law of nature, it shall break us. Harmony with nature ceases and humanity then gets to learn the law of cause and effect, known in the East as karma. It is up to all of us to create

a new culture by not breaking the laws of nature. We must make new choices, without compromise. We must leave the Earth better than we found it. Pure air is one of those choices.

What we are addressing here is a state of consciousness. In one state there is guardianship and care of the Earth. In the other, there is dishonor, disrespect and blatant lack of reverence for the Earth and our harmony with all of nature.

We must shift now or we shall pay an even bigger price of violating the balance as we already have with global warming issues, the disappearance of millions of honey bees and many of the pollinators and the list goes on.

We must clearly want to know the truth. We must want to know the right thing to do here. It can have nothing to do with politics, with business, with economics. It is clear that there is a higher principle that must be recognized when deciding the action that must be lived here in Northern California and across the nation and the globe. Our elements of water, earth and air must be deeply valued. The value of purity must be made a priority.

Together…we can stop this crime against nature.
Together…we can build a new culture.
Together…we can give a VOICE to the living element air.
We are one family.
Together…we can do this.

I thank you for this consideration and for the call for truth.

* This passage came in the night and was presented at a California hearing on clean air.

Respond to Inner Vision

"Let us each respond to inner Vision,
rather than react to the outer world…
of miscreations borne of human false
concepts and the battle of duality."

It is often very difficult to not be swept up in the "outer seeming of the appearance world." I say unto you that the "world is within." There is nothing but Consciousness in all the Universe. Whether we stay in and "react" to the outer human consciousness of the battle of duality of the ever human scene, that is of the finite sense, is up to us.

Until we go ever deeper, we will be living "in reaction" to what appears to be human power given always to someone or something external. For the moment, it is feeling victim to a political party with its beliefs. Tomorrow it will be something else. This is all a human state of misidentification and feeling the pain of that misidentification.

There is only One Power and it is the Power of the Infinite. Each of us that goes within and allows that One Power to give us vision can go into action Now. Each precious soul has a Vision to be Lived in Action…Now. The Mystical as the Practical…Now. The presidential elections perhaps have changed one thing…the desire in each to go ever deeper within into the Realm of the Real. Feel the ecstasy of the realm of the real.

There is much more Light/Consciousness on the planet than ever before. That light shines through those who open to the Light. We are that very Light. We can only allow it to live through us as love, wisdom, beauty and all the other supreme qualities. With more Light, those things that break the universal Law of Balance, that is the law of love, do surface to be released. We cannot waver when those things that break the Law of Love do surface to be released. It is good. They are exposed. We must put them in the light of love. My book, *The Holy Sight,* was written to assist in this very matter, unto these very times.

This is not a time to give power to duality of parties, duality of genders, duality of anything. The One Power knows opposites but not opposition. It is one. Duality is the realm of endless and painful battle of oppositions and karma, devoid of grace. Let us be empowered by the Vision of the One Power. Let us allow this Consciousness to reveal to us our script, our actions, our expressions and responses of the supreme creativity, this supreme love and wisdom, which married…bears beauty.

This is not a time to "outline" to Supreme Consciousness what we want and cry like children if we do not get it. This is a time to allow that Consciousness of Oneness to live in us, through us, around us and as us.

This is not a time to give power to the finite universe. This is a time to quit externalizing power and authority, whether in government, spiritual matters or in the home. This is a time to finally be in that lifetime that one finds revealed within the Self…direct knowing.

Away Tey Ewa Tey.
Now is the Time.

Direct knowing, friends. It is a time for direct knowing. Any one of us could turn the tides, for "the within IS the without," the "as above IS the below." There is no separation. Listen, like never before, and do what is ours to do in this beautiful and precious "play of creation." Do not "act" like breaking the inviolate and inexorable Law of Love has any power. The Power is within.

Allow It to live through us. We are the precious vessels of Infinity.
We must not then act like victims of the "outer seeming!"
Let us take responsibility for becoming the "birther of new forms,"
Birthers of a new culture.
The ancient meaning of culture is…gathering of light.
It really does not matter who is president for us to do this.
We are the higher Consciousness unfolding, expanding.
Let us be aware and do this now. It is time.

There is a growing multitude of us that has opened to the "light of knowing."
Let that Light of Knowing be the direct revelation of our every moment.
Let us live in the ecstasy of that Knowing, not in the false identification and reaction to the outer world. This is our moment to know that.

Reality is within and we are the instruments through which it manifests and materializes in the physical universe.

Let us be the example of that.

Each moment…let us radiate that knowing.

Let us not need or expect others to "change" the world. Each Consciousness of each human that aligns with the One Mind, the One Power…will know what is theirs to do.

Let us begin this day…to leave "reaction to the outer world"…

Let us respond to the Vision given to us from the One Self, our True Self, from within…

Let our Actions be borne of Vision…the grand "presider" is within…

Written just after G.W. Bush was elected for a second time. The message is pertinent for all times, not just this election.

A Message unto these Times

Humanity is awakening out of a long sleep in duality, a sense of separation from Spirit, Light. We may end this slumbering that has created endless fear and suffering. We may shift our awareness to the Presence of Light, to the Consciousness we already are, beneath the wall of beliefs. We may breathe in the Light, the carrier of love and wisdom, that is everywhere present and "feel" it. It is who we are. We "feel" it in our heart as the light being within. Pure Love. This world is within.

Awaken to that and our outer world…it changes. The Changeless One manifest as the ever changing world of form. Interrelated. The Dance of the One. The One come as the Many: one and the same.

Let us now open to this holy sight for our Self and we will open to the holy sight (sacred vision) for everyone, everyplace and all of Nature. We experience holy relationship with all. We are aware and experience the One that we are. We enter a new world. We enter the Timeless Realm…and it is Love.

Now…it is…that we see the wholeness…that already is. Now…it is…that we see the true identity of all.

Awa Tey Ewa Tey…Now is the Time.

A Field of Knowing: The Soul's Knowing...of Sacred Placement and Sacred Space

As a child, it seemed to me that a portion of my world was a hell world. So I began to weave magic space and to live in my own world.

Awakening was happening. I did not even know it.

I was in junior high in the Rio Grande Valley of Texas. My parents were pilots with the air force and when they were home they mainly fought and drank. Some of the fighting was in silence; that was the worst, because everyone had to pretend it was not happening and yet everybody knew. I knew they were alcoholics and I found my innocent and childlike way of relating to the world in a sacred way. I created my own world of sacred placement and space.

Cigarettes, ash trays, beer cans littered the homes we lived in, leaving smells I did not like, as we traveled from air base to air base. When no one was present, I would begin to move things around. I could easily find "placement" that just simply felt good. It was innate. It never occurred to me that others were not living from that place. I would be elated with the wonderful change in how the room felt. I did not know the words sacred or shift of energy then. It would be many years before I developed a language for what came so naturally. But, without a doubt, I possessed a keen awareness of what "rooms" felt like. Years later, I discovered it was an acute spiritual sensitivity.

Most of my time growing up I had to share a bedroom

with an older sister who was messy (by my standards) in her keeping of our room. I would demand that we have distinctly separate sides because I loved the "feeling" in my side of the room. We did not have much money or many things, but I cherished what I had and cared for it as if it were worth a fortune. I would practice sacred placement and position my little things that a child does collect. I had an innate feeling for how to create a space that at least I could feel good in.

I continued to become acutely aware of space and how I felt when I was in it. My father, being a violent, angry and invasive alcoholic taught me (unknowingly to him) many wonderful things. It would take me many years to see the gifts I was given. It would take me years to see the tools provided for rapid soul growth. I learned quickly that the space around my father was often dangerous in almost every way. It serves no purpose to to go into the lurid details of how it was dangerous, especially for a girl. But it does serve to say that I "awoke to space." There was space that was filled with good feelings and there was space that was filled with all kinds of negative feelings. Unsafe, insecure, fearful, dangerous, intimidating and abusive and on. Strange that I never took it personally. And I did not like it.

I learned, for the most part, to be invisible in space that did not feel good. Then I would immediately find ways to my "feel good spaces."

I will digress a moment. Before my mother died, she wanted me to know something about my childhood. She said that for the first three years of my life that I simply sat on a little stool in the middle of the room with my eyes open, staring and smiling into space. I did not speak. She said that I never caused any problems and was always happy. She said if she told me it was naptime, that I just laid down and smiled at her and fell asleep. She was aware that it was not what was considered normal behavior, but she said she decided not to tell others, as during that historical period, people were put in mental institutions for even what was considered slight abnormalities. She said she felt I was a happy being. She said it was a joy to be in my space.

By four years old, I had found the out of doors. I had found nature. I was not to be found much of the time. And the family was simply too dysfunctional to care where I was or even to notice. For many years, I suffered for the lack of caring and grew to feel great self-pity. It was many years later that I discovered the beauty and gifts given to me during the time of such huge freedom to discover nature, without the normal conditioning that was happening to the young people around me. First, I found the ecstasy of the feeling of space and spaciousness in nature. I spent much time wildly climbing trees and then would find the best space in the tree for being. (I did not know words such as meditation or contemplative prayer.) I was in such joy. I could feel the calm of nature. There was no one to scream, be angry, hit or be mean to me or others in the family. Like a military sergeant.

None of this existed in the purity of the sacred space of nature. I learned to place myself where it felt safe and secure and loving and peace filled. I found myself placing myself on community water towers, high piles of lumber in lumber yards (leaping from one to the next), on the roof of the garage (trying to fly with a sheet) and on great old tree vines flying over deep ravines in Mississippi. Always…a great sense of freedom.

In these instances, it was not outside objects that were being placed. It was me. I was placing myself in places that were joyful and free. I loved it. I loved finding these places.

I even found a space behind the bushes lining my grandparents' huge Victorian home; there I would find money. I would take a tablespoon from the kitchen out to this sacred and abundant space and begin to dig in the earth. Treasures appeared. I would find dimes, nickels and quarters. I never did know how this treasure got there. I just believed and it was there. I bought lollipops I wanted from the small Iowa town candy store.

Once I married, I began to find again how much I loved it when I was all alone in the house. I loved it. The joy was so great that I never even considered that something might not be normal in my deep love of solitude. I had found sanctuary. Again, this was years before I began to meditate in a formal way.

I could just begin to feel what furniture, art or vases, etc. wanted to shift and move. It would not have even been shocking during this period if the objects just began to speak to me and told me where they wanted to be. Even plants would convey to me the message of where they wanted to be. The things in the rooms seemed to be communicating with me. However, during this time, I was just mindlessly doing what I could feel so clearly. I seemed to have an innate ability to be a part of this constantly moving scene in my home. A great upliftment would come as I followed this intuition that spoke blatantly to me.

I remember meeting many other women. They would talk of ideas from designers, magazines and space systems they were using. I would be horrified at the idea of losing the freedom to "feel" the sacred space and placement. I also could not understand why these women did not want to listen to themselves in finding sacred placement and creating sacred space. It all seemed so obvious to me. And it was never a sense of a static idea that was to remain that way in the room.

My home was becoming a living book of changes. I loved it.

Whether I was hitchhiking in Europe or on a private bus across the Middle East or on a third class train in India, I continued to have a growing awareness of my place and the placement of objects that were in my charge. Once I began to meditate, this was no longer just a vague intuition or a sense of rightness; it became a definite field of knowing.

I began to draw during this time and this amazing sense of placement continued with the figures I was drawing.

The years passed. As inspirational ideas for paintings, jewelry, sculpture and ceremonial cactus gardens came to me, I found myself placing symbols and nature objects everywhere about my home. I came to call this spontaneous sacred living ceremony, never to be repeated or cloned again. Life as Living Ceremony.

I became aware that there were many spiritual systems that had rigid sacred placement. I considered studying some of these systems. But I trusted when they just did not feel like the path I was on. So I just went right on with this powerful inner impulse toward conscious sacred placement of myself and the objects that were in my trust. In that, sacred space happened. I always felt I was looking over the things in my life.

As long as it was in my safekeeping, I honored and respected it. It did not feel like it was a possession. Rather I was its guardian.

Finally in 1981, while I was meditating, I had an ancient remembering. I had visions of times and lives and cultures past where I was dancing. I was dancing and could only be regarded as a temple tender and a temple dancer. I was home.

All that I had been remembering and intuiting, since a child, was revealed in inner vision. It all had been opening to me. It all now was making sense.

As a temple tender, I held sacred space. The space was free of clutter and unnecessary things. The space was free of negative thoughts and people who did not stay in resonance with the divine.

Sacred placement in the temple was not static. The placing of the Self was a dance. Dancing through space kept the energy clear. Beauty reigned. Love ruled.

As an artist, I know how art supplies can be everyplace in a studio. And in an art studio that sense of sacred space is very strong. What it looks like through each artist as they dance through space is individual and unique. There is not a system. There is not a formula for this dance. It is living. It is breathing, spontaneous and ever changing. It is life itself. It is a mindless dance as inspiration pours through from Infinity.

Thus, these bleedthroughs from other lives and other places do find their way into our lives.

What I would love to share here is how to get out of the human mental mind constructs and systems. I would love to extend the invitation to come into the no-mind. Unfortunately this is often considered impractical and unwanted and even dyslexic in our society.

This no-mind is the One Mind that is Creator ever awaiting the giving forth of creative ideas. I would even venture to say that the human mind is clever, but not Creative in this sense. This True and Original Creative Principle extends to us in the pineal and effervesces into our consciousness and body. Our brain is the willing servant of such brilliant and glowing ideas and visions.

In this manner, we can leave forever the human mental rules that would hold us in painful bondage. Deeply feel this place of no system, no formula, no rigidity. Allow that feeling of such freedom of being to permeate every cell, to permeate consciousness. Allow the feeling of direct knowing. Allow no separation between consciousness and Consciousness. Divine Consciousness manifest as your consciousness. One and the same.

Then…it is…that every moment takes on the scintillation of sacred placement. It does not matter if it is your placement in a room or your placement of a painting, a chair, a rug. Listen inwardly. Truly…the Word…it comes. It comes often unheard, yet heard. It comes even softly in the night. It comes heralding the joy of knowing. It comes revealing how to trust. And soul growth bursts forth…

Sacred placement is synonymous with rapture. For to carry out sacred placement, one must be open and receptive to this inflow of divine consciousness. The heart knows joy.

I struggled for a moment of whether to use only generic words in this description. However, it comes to me that human pleasure and Rapture are not closely related. One leaves you with longing for the next human pleasure, even attached to it. The other leaves one with upliftment and fulfillment. It deeply satisfies. Generic just does not have all the flavors and possibilities. Infinite possibilities is the state of consciousness that is practiced in the creating of sacred space and placement.

One may ask how to practice creating sacred space and applying sacred placement.

I have known of many to pay others to help them get rid of certain feelings in their homes, be it endless chaotic clutter, unused items and just great outer confusion. Some people do not yet see the connection between the inner lives and their outer lives. It is a very powerful and enlightening experience of soul growth to do this fully alone. There is no one to lean on or depend on. No one to defer to. No one to play the "I don't know" game with. It is just Divine Presence manifest as you. That is it. One has to ask, to open and to receive. After a while those three steps just dissolve into the dance of knowing and acting. And joy…it is there…

You may use this awareness of sacred placement to assist in the creation of sacred space for anything in your home. There are no rules. You are delighting with the dance of all that is in your field. You are playing as purely as a child. And no formulas. Practice feeling the rightness. You will know. You are not awaiting someone's rigid system of right and wrong. You are open and receptive.

The Infinite is dancing through you. And you allow. Rapture fills your every cell in such simple movements, in such simple placements. Here and there, when you open to direct knowing from within, you "feel It." That is It! In this moment, that is It!

The feeling begins to grow. You continue to try this out in more and more areas in your life. Leave nothing out. Allow your imagination.

Notice even when you arrive at a gathering of any sort. Instead of using your mind to figure out where to go, allow the awareness of the perfection of sacred placement to come into your consciousness. Feel where to be and who to join. Or even who not to join. One opens to the ineffable. The unspeakable does speak. Social rules do flee.

Every instance does begin to be living. Even the finding of a place to park your car. One need not try to get one. Or even affirm, pray or petition to get one. Just open to receive the perfect space. Your sacred placement is awaiting your awareness. Each moment of life becomes the ecstasy of practicing this Sacred Space and Placement.

Look at every room and every corner and every object. Feel! Feel if it is in its right place. Trust. You will know.

Practice this! Practice this each day until you are just doing it.

This consciousness that you are practicing is the Infinite Consciousness. It is literally the substance of creation. As the living substance of creation, it is your abundance, your supply, your everything. This includes your knowing of sacred placement in order to create sacred space.

This is not always easy. There is no book to open. There are no rigid rules. There is no person to call. No workshop to attend. There is always only the Self. And that Self is yourself, if it is in unity and oneness with the One Self.

The grandest Designer of all can live through you and as you. Open to it. Listen to it. Allow it. Be in gratitude to it. And feel it.

It is creative. Never again do you need to say "I am not the creative type." It simply is not true. We all are creative as we merge with the One.

In 1988, just over two years after I built a small home overlooking Mount Shasta, I was prompted from within to begin creating ceremonial sculptures and later ceremonial cactus gardens complete with kachinas, archetypal figures, crystals, stones, feathers, candles, sage, sticks and beaded jewelry. Whatever I happened to find out hiking in nature, such as animal bones and plant roots, were also becoming primordial and sacred ceremonies in the gardens. I even turned much of my dining room into a cactus garden, so that I could easily choose whatever cactus I wanted.

Now I was awakening to a new awareness. This sacred placement and space was becoming something that I could joyfully share with others. I avoided promoting and marketing and allowed people to find this magic.

Awareness filled me as I created each one. I was holding space for Beauty. I have grown to experience Beauty as the living expression of the marriage of love and wisdom. Yin and Yang. In balance. Beauty is the walk of balance upon this Earth. And it lives in us all to express. This was simply another avenue through which I could give love and form a body.

Allow yourself to find ever new and fully unexplored ways to use this practice of sacred placement.

Since 1971, I began to scan the globe in my consciousness, feeling for places that I would like to visit or even live. The places that turn up in your consciousness may be fully different than anything you have ever imagined.

Roam freely in the spaciousness of your consciousness to feel and know the locations that seem to glow for you. I have known way too many people who say, "I can't do that. I do not have the money." Or "I don't know how I could do that." Notice here the limiting thought of "I don't know" or "I don't have." Those thoughts then become the consciousness that does manifest. They are barriers of steel to your imagination and dreams. Remember that Consciousness/ Source/ Cause/ God is the very center of your being. And It is your supply. It will feed you, clothe you and create travel. It is the Ultimate Space. It is spaciousness that is vast and infinite. This consciousness is your supply. Open and allow it to come to you in the form needed in this day. Be in gratitude. And it will grow. Go to Cause and the effects in this physical world may manifest from a realm of divine creation. Otherwise we appear or seem to be victims of circumstances and other people who think they know better than we our movement through space.

During the time that I was raising my two daughters, I did my best to allow them to create sacred space in their rooms. I made many mistakes. I remember telling one daughter that she could not paint her room black. My own limitations came flooding in. But most of the time they were able to use their own knowing.

Storytelling has become my vehicle to describe how each of us carries within us this sense of Beauty…which is Sacred Space. And once one can give it to the Self, then one can share with another. Presence is everywhere, but without conscious Presence it is like an unused Aladdin's Lamp. It becomes conscious when we are aware of it and when we feel it. Western civilization has practically snuffed out the arts that nurture and cultivate sensitivity and the ability to feel.

This growing sense of sacred space did find a way to go beyond the imaginings of my mind in 1981. I went into a nine hour meditation in which I broke fully through the human mind and expanded in consciousness out into the universe and star systems. I expanded past teachers and teachings and experienced for this brief glimpse the purity of I Am Awareness. I experienced the Divine Mind as a Oneness. Awareness permeated me, that this included all, regardless of all the differences of beliefs. This moment of mysticism opened up an entirely new awareness of Sacred Space. We as a humanity have life awaiting us beyond any mental conception or belief. We can open to it.

....

I told a friend this story of my awakening to sacred space and placement as a young girl. She said it reminded her of the opening of a lotus. She said that it was as if each experience of awakening opened another petal of illumination.

It was slow. It was gradual. I did not see the aerial view of this unfolding realization. I only knew that I needed the space to be myself. I needed the space to listen within to the center of my being, which as a child, had no name.

Only in that deep listening did I know what to do.

When I was with a husband or a boyfriend, it was the most difficult for me. I could feel and sense all their desires, wants and needs. And what my soul was speaking was somehow lost in the static. My own self's knowing was buried in living the life of another's life whose purpose was different from mine. It is no wonder that so many women are clinging to men. Actually the men should have compassion, for the woman has set her own soul aside and merged with another. She cannot even find herself.

Doctors...please...
no more death sentences

Why is it you continue to lure innocent, trusting people that become your knowing or unknowing victims, into your snares, a death sentence? All of the public knows that you give hours, days, weeks, months and sometimes years to live. The public knows that you tell people to "get their affairs" in order. The public, for now, still mainly believes you.

You, doctors, become Death calling.

Why do you do this? Do you really believe your sentence given to others? Were you taught to do this in medical school? Does it give you a sense of power to call the shots for another's life?

Or is it simply that you have no faith? No inner knowing yet that "all is possible?" Have you not yet heard enough stories of people that lived anyway? Have you not heard the stories of the people who defied physical plane statistics and lived on? Have you not tired of feeding the public your beliefs? Have you not tired of the sadness, the suffering that you do bring? And the false beliefs built on a monumental belief in separation from the Source.

small purple butterfly
lands upon my left writing hand

Have you not wondered how some of your patients healed anyway? They lived. They walked. They found the way.

Have you not wondered how they survived? Do you really believe they were misdiagnosed?

Have not their stories of "living" touched your heart and soul?

Why have you ignored these messages? Or sneered? Or just acted like you did not want to hear or know.

Did you know the stories of your ignoring (ignorance) are shared among the people?

Many of the simple people know that anything is possible. Many simple and commonsense people know they do not need to buy the "claim of death's premature clutches."

The world now grows, evolves, changes.
Please do join in this emerging culture.
Here, infinite possibilities do dwell.

Tell me now…how do we have the changing of the seasons? How do the stars move with grace across the sky?

Tell me now…have you glimpsed life everlasting? Or do your beliefs cause it to ever elude you?

Here is another subject of which the people of the street do speak. They speak of the high suicide rates of doctors in the medical profession.

Tell me now…how can that be? You who are trained to be the giver of lives. How did this happen?

What classes or understandings are not in your classroom curriculums of attaining the letters D and r? And have you even asked the questions? Who or what might have made sure that was not part of the teaching? Was it ignorance or was it deliberate? Ask to know.

I tell you we enter now a new sphere of influence.
I tell you that you are invited into new lands.
I tell you now that you must open to new ways.

I tell you now that you must call on the Changeless One that brings the change. Call IT whatever scientific or medical name that fits for you. Whatever it is that you call IT, ask to feel IT, to experience IT. Ask It to enlighten you. It is Life Itself.

Very soon, gone shall be the days of death sentences given by our doctors under the Hippocratic oath to bring no harm.

I tell you...the death sentence does bring harm. It brings harm in the form of suffering and potential premature deaths.

Be a bringer of this change. You will touch the medical profession far and wide.

Those who survive the death sentences are not miracle people. They simply have entered, through receptivity, another frequency of life.

This has been an immense game of belief and/or power. If you want to see power, open to Power, the One Power. Distance yourself from the belief in two powers. Human and the way of the Nameless One. There is no twoness except as belief.

Humble yourself and be the vessel through which the Power that is Life may flow.

Allow your profession to be honorable.

The medical profession assists in emergencies and does save many lives. That is honorable.

And there are areas of great concern by the public that are not honorable. Giving mainly toxic medications is harmful. It is the antithesis of "do not harm" that is part of your oath.

Perhaps begin to humble yourself to the sacred essence that lives as the plant kingdom. And do not desecrate it with toxic additives. A little history does reveal that the ancients and the natives and indigenous peoples around the world have known the plant kingdom and the power that runs through it. It grows freely.

You claim to be brilliant, some of the highest IQs in the world. Please use this brilliance to serve the true ways. Ways that are organic. Ways that do not harm. Ways that do not have detrimental side effects. Side effects that are harm filled. Why do you agree to live in this lie?

Humanity is at a crossroads, much like the ancient Atlantis and Lemuria. That crossroads is a choice point. It is a choice of heart or human mind. It is a choice of truth or lies. It is a choice of true healing and wholeness or endless dependence on drugs and medications to grow the wealth of a self-appointed few. It is a choice of balance or imbalance for the world. It is a choice of a sick humanity or "physician, heal thyself."

Your choice may assist to help with this collective global shift into Consciousness that we are One.

No longer shall the few be important.
No longer shall the few carry all the gold.
And most important, no longer shall the death sentences have power.
The era is at an end.

Do come.
Bring your colleagues.
Teach them.
Inspire them.
Invite them.

Awa Tey Ewa Tey
Now is the Time

Written at the Northfork on May 20, 2012,
on the Annular Eclipse day at 3:15 p.m.

The title of this had begun to come several days before the writing.

NOTE: It is known that many doctors are not like this and have made the shift long ago. Gratitude fills those who see and are living the changes.

The World is in You

Friends, oh friends. The world is in you...I say...
*   the world is in you.*
Gazing out into creation...one does imagine
*   the opposite is true...*
I weep to see collections of world's forms...
*   turning already into ashes...as*
*   the clock does tick away...*
Bringing tears of sorrow and despair...when
*   nothing is left within the grasp of hand...*

Come fly with me...another world does wait...
*   its precious contents elude your very eye...*
*   yet it stands waiting to be seen...*
Sublime...oh how sublime...it dances
*   outside the reaches of your mind...*
The mind inquires upon its life long search
*   what never can be found inside itself...*
Yea...there is no valley of death...
*   but in the mind...*

Behold...this other world...
Sweetly does it sing from every flower...from
*   every crawling snail...*
Behold this song...it is the world...
It is the world...inside of you...

About the Artist/Writer

Mystic artist/writer, Mary Saint-Marie was led by a dream to the mountains of Northern California in 1974. She has lived close to nature since that time.

Mary Saint-Marie's Art of the Soul has been viewed at more than 150 exhibits, in galleries, expositions, conferences, faires and workshops across the country. It has been shown at workshops in Europe. Mary's art is in private art collections around the world. The visionary art has been featured on TV interviews and in books and magazines.

The Animating Presence is the seventh published book by Mary. She also has two CDs that may be viewed on her website. *Journey of Consciousness* is a meditation and *Soul Sounds of World Birth* is soul sounding as a portal into presence.

Mary performed for seven years in multi-media enactments called *SHE…it is …who Remembers* with her art, narration, soul sounding, dancing and music. In 2010 Mary produced a play that she wrote, via a dream. *The Monitor and Laughter of the Gods* is the story of balance of the masculine and feminine principle. It is sacred theatre providing Awareness of our Oneness.

Please visit the websites at:
www.MarySaintMarie.com
www.EarthCareGlobalTV.com

Fine art reproductions of art are available to order.
Books may be ordered through www.Amazon.com

Mary Saint-Marie also is a spiritual educator. She shares through Soul Sessions, Soul Retreats and The Holy Sight Workshops.

www.ingramcontent.com/pod-product-compliance
Lightning Source LLC
LaVergne TN
LVHW051123080426
835510LV00018B/2198